Winners Are
RESPECTFUL

Life Source Scholars

Grades TK-2nd

Winners are Respectful

Written by the scholars of Life Source International Charter school grades Tk-2nd May 2017.

Published by:
Affirmative Expression
PO Box 360856
Decatur, GA 30036

First edition copyright © 2017, Affirmative Expression

All rights reserved. No part of this book may be reproduced or transmitted in any form or by any means, electronic or mechanical, including photocopying, recording, or by any information storage or retrieval system, without written permission of the author.

Cover by Chelsey Thomas
chels.t14@gmail.com

Printed in the United States of America

ISBN: **978-0-9963605-3-1**

Letter from the Publisher

The Anthology Project is a program created to provide a platform for voices to be heard. Often times youth feel their voices are not valuable. Others may feel pressure from the concern of their work being good enough for a passing grade. But while participating in this collaborative project they are able to speak freely with no concern for whether they will pass or fail. Most importantly, through the support of readers like you, their voices, stories, and efforts are validated and for that I thank you.

Tierica Berry
CEO
A Woman's Standard

FOREWORD

When I created the Anthology Project it was to shed light on the voice of today's youth as it relates to various topics. Over the past few months I have had the honor and pleasure of working with the scholars of Life Source International Charter School.

These scholars were asked what respect is and how we show it. During dialogue about this topic they were able to come together and write this book:

Winners are Respectful

Enjoy.

♥

Tierica Berry

CONTENTS

1 Ms. Calderon   Pg 1

2 Ms. Katambwe   Pg 23

3 Ms. Richards   Pg 37

4 Ms. Castro   Pg 87

ACKNOWLEDGMENTS

Before we begin special thanks must be giving to the people that made this anthology project possible.

Dr. Culpepper for seeing the vision and bringing the Anthology Project to Life Source.

Mr. Mix because under his guidance the project has been steered in the right direction.

The front office staff **Ms. Powers, Ms. Padilla, and Ms. Lopez** for helping to manage some of the fine details of this project.

Mr. Howard for assistance in scheduling.

Mrs. Mix for planning the book signing.

Last but certainly not least special thanks to the classroom **teachers** that worked closely with the scholars to complete their writing submissions. Without you this book would not be possible.

On behalf of Affirmative Expression and the student authors,
Thank You!

CHAPTER 1
CALDERON

Anonymous

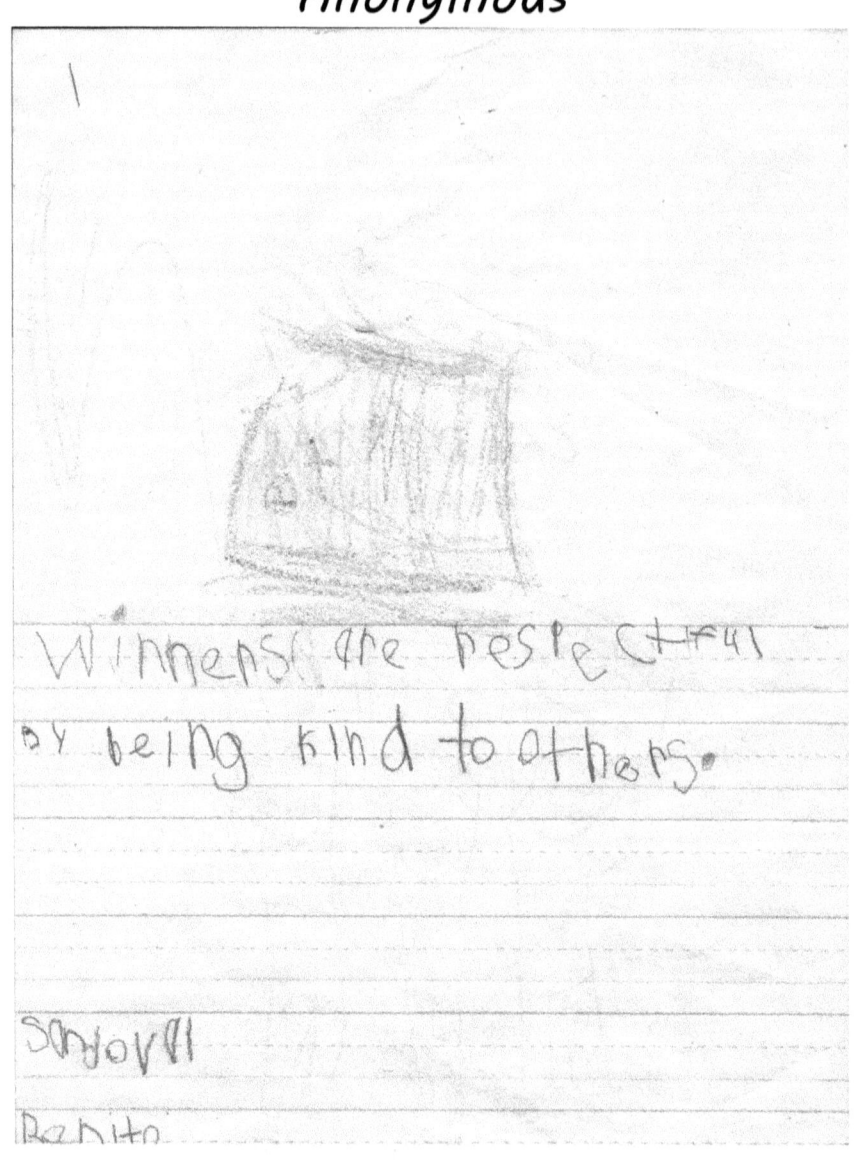

Winners are respectful by being kind to others.

Sonyovel
Benito

Male
Grade: TK

Anonymous

Winners are respectful when they share.

Grade: TK

Anonymous

Winners are respctfu when they share.

Female
Grade: TK

Winners are Respectful

Anonymous

Winnerare
respectel
Weanthevs

Grade: TK

Anonymous

Winners are resEctful when they share

Grade: TK

Anonymous

Female
Grade: TK

Anonymous

Female

Grade: TK

Angelo

Winners are respec
When they sh

Male
Grade: TK

Anonymous

Winners are respectful when they share.

Female
Grade: TK

Anonymous

Grade: TK

Janae

Female
Grade: TK

Tommie

Male
Grade: TK

Anonymous

Winners are
when the wait
reg it respectful

Female
Grade: TK

Keimon

Winners are
With are not
By being kind

Male
Grade: TK

Anonymous

Winners are respectful when the wait their turn

Female
Grade: TK

Janae

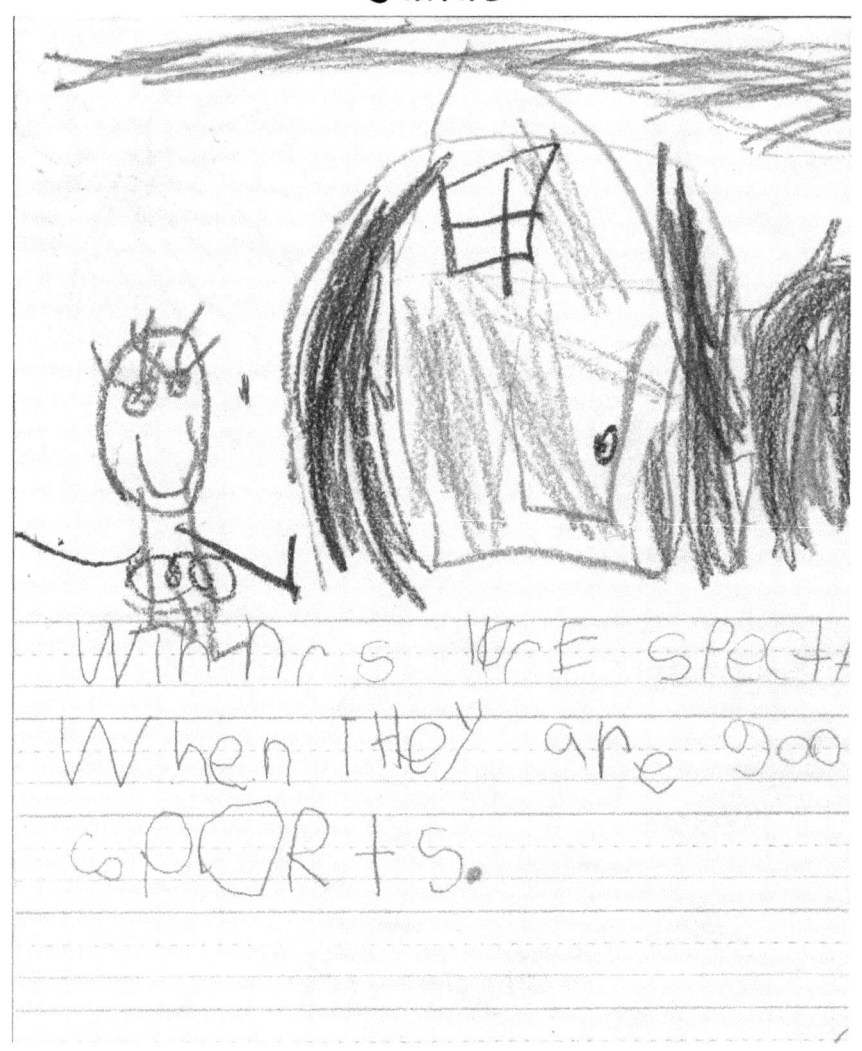

Female

Grade: TK

Anonymous

Winners are respectful when they are good sports.

Grade: TK

Anonymous

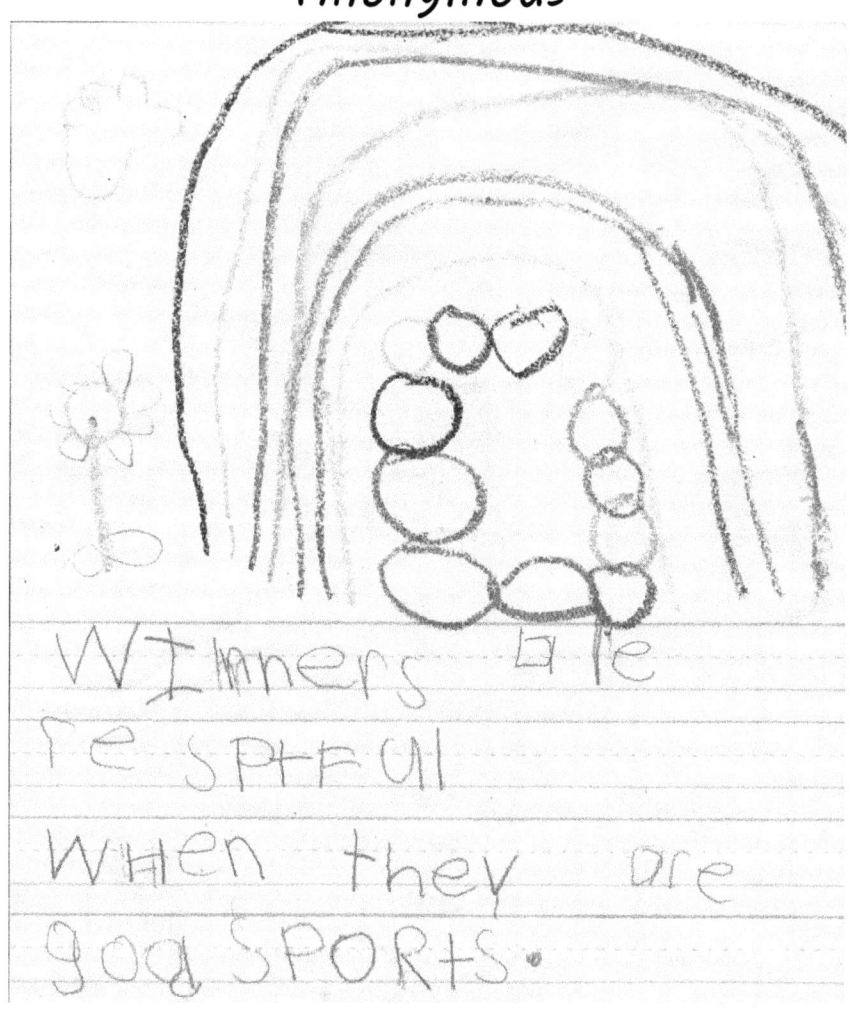

Winners are resptful when they are god sports.

Female
Grade: TK

Gabrielle

Winners are respectful by being kind to others

Female
Grade: TK

Anonymous

Female

Grade: TK

CHAPTER 2
Katambwe

ABRAHAM

Male
Grade: Kindergarten

Olivia

I take turns at the play ground.

Female
Grade: Kindergarten

Brooklyn

Female
Grade: Kindergarten

Sebastian

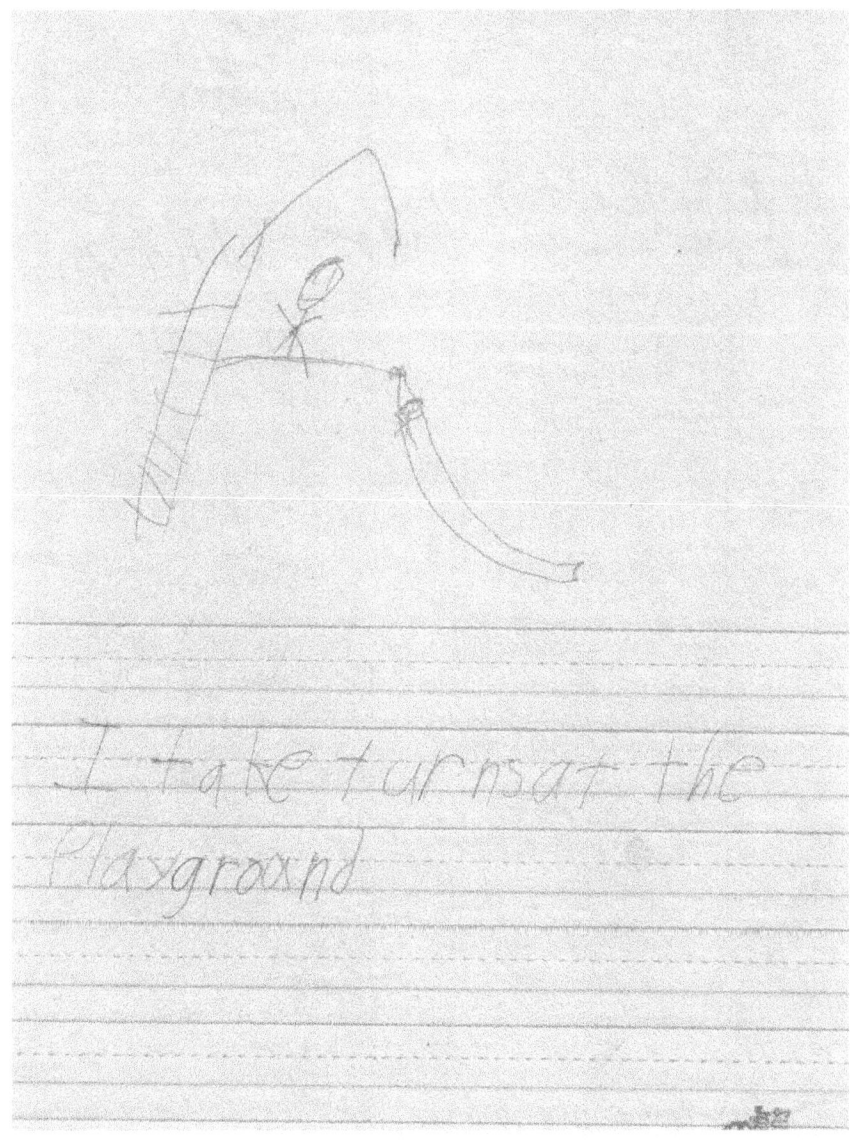

Male

Grade: Kindergarten

Kaliah

Female
Grade: Kindergarten

Keynon

Male
Grade: Kindergarten

Aahleiah-Anne Mahree

Female
Grade: Kindergarten

Winners are Respectful

Jymie-Lee

Female

Grade: Kindergarten

Vondell

Male
Grade: Kindergarten

Winners are Respectful

Kerri

Female

Grade: Kindergarten

Jissett

I share with my friends on the swing.

Female
Grade: Kindergarten

Jo'Siyah

Male
Grade: Kindergarten

CHAPTER 3
Richards

Aaron

I show respect by
helping others.
I'm respecting chores
and listening.
By Aaron

Male
Grade: 1st Grade

Abigail

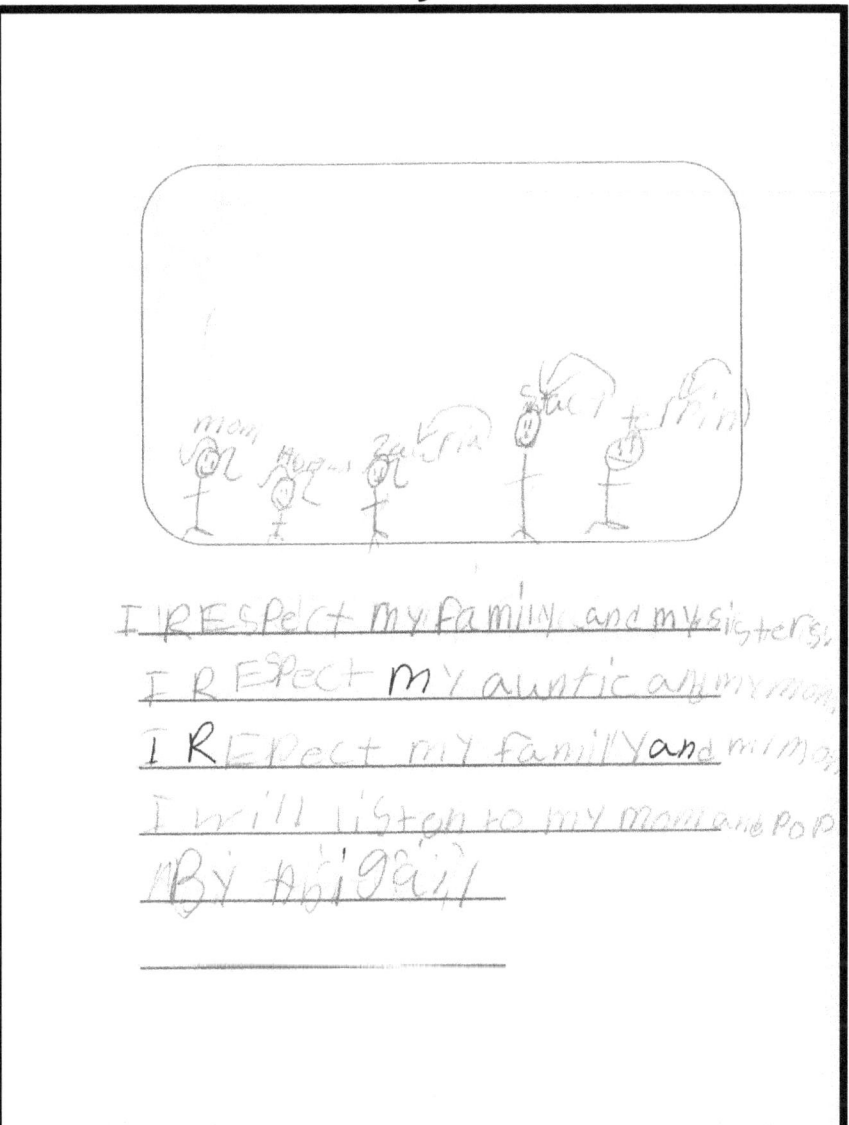

I RESPect my family and my sisters.
I REPect my auntie and my mom.
I REPect my family and mimo.
I will listen to my mom and Pop
By Abigail

Female
Grade: 1st Grade

Allisson

I show respect by helping teachers and others. Respect means being nice. By: Allisson

Female
Grade: 1st Grade

Bryan

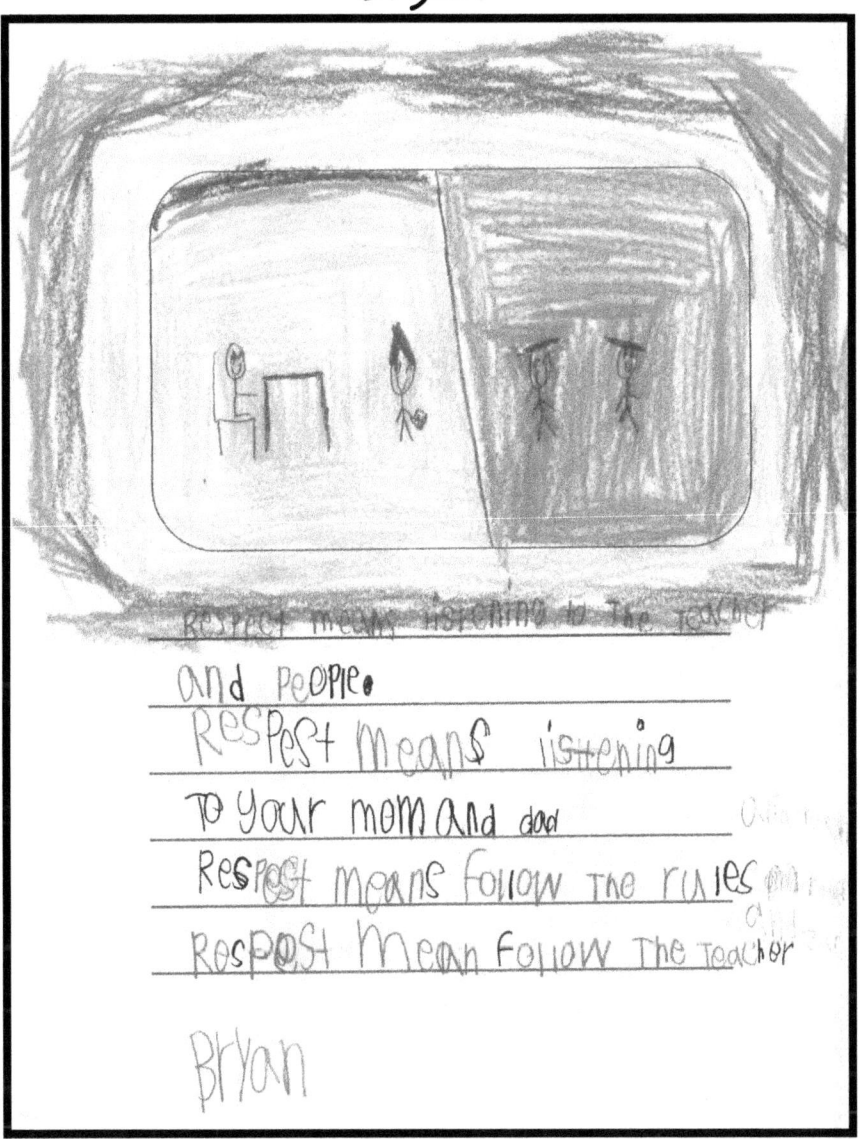

Male

Grade: 1st Grade

Caiden

from caiden

I show respect by follwing the rwls and by helping my mom do dishes.

Male
Grade: 1st Grade

Danny

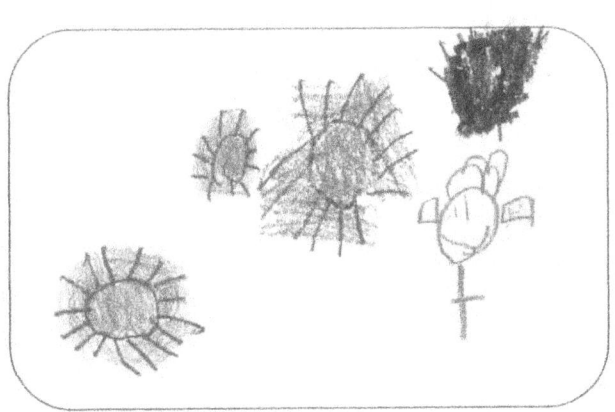

Respect means listening to the rules. I show respect for the teacher.
by DANNY

Male
Grade: 1st Grade

Chance

Respect means to be kind to others.
Respect means to be a nice someone.
Respect means to help someone when they fall.
By chance

Male
Grade: 1st Grade

Darrion

Respect means follow directions quickly and listen to your teacher. Respect also means listen to your mom and dad.
by Darrion

Male
Grade: 1st Grade

Demaje

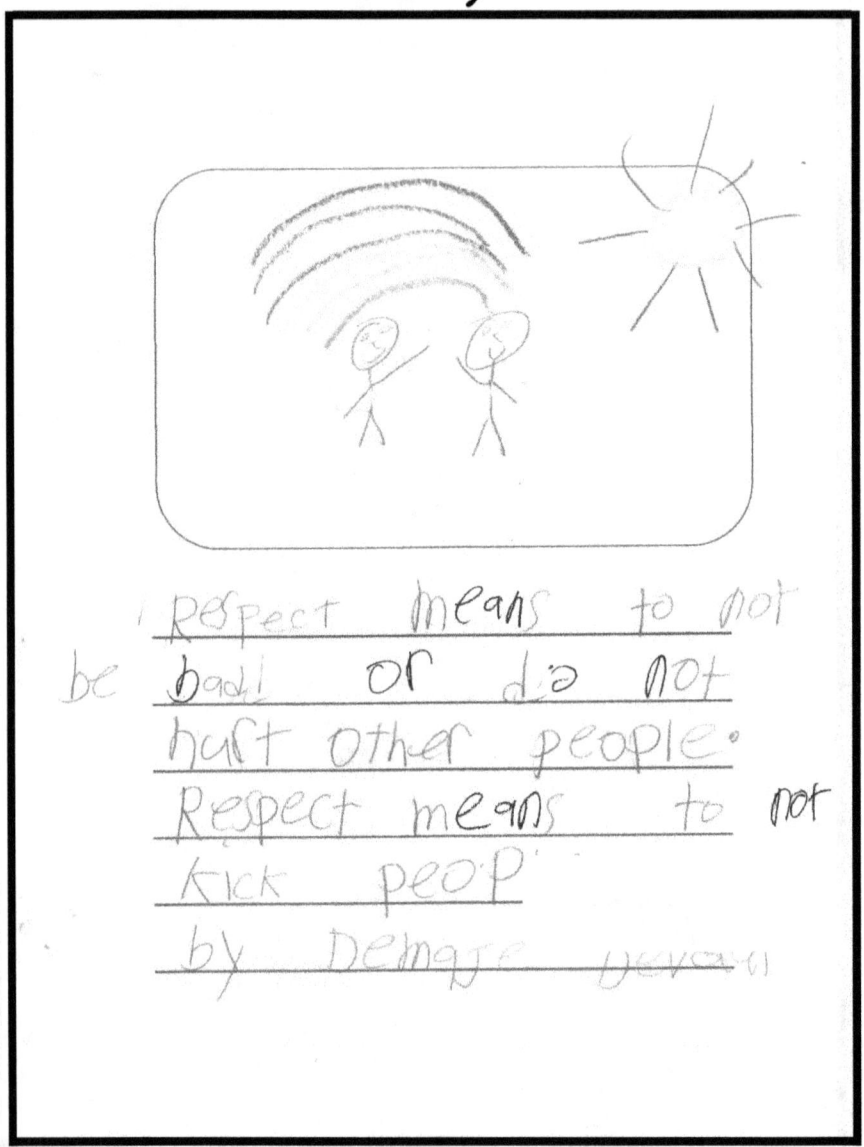

Respect means to not be bad or do not hurt other people. Respect means to not kick peop' by Demaje

Female

Grade: 1st Grade

DeAndre

I show respect by being good at school and listening to my teacher.
By DeAndre

Male
Grade: 1st Grade

Diore

I show respect by helping my grahdma get in the car. one time my grahdma fell and I went to go get my daddy andmem to help and a good thing that I had help

Name Diore

Female
Grade: 1st Grade

E.C.

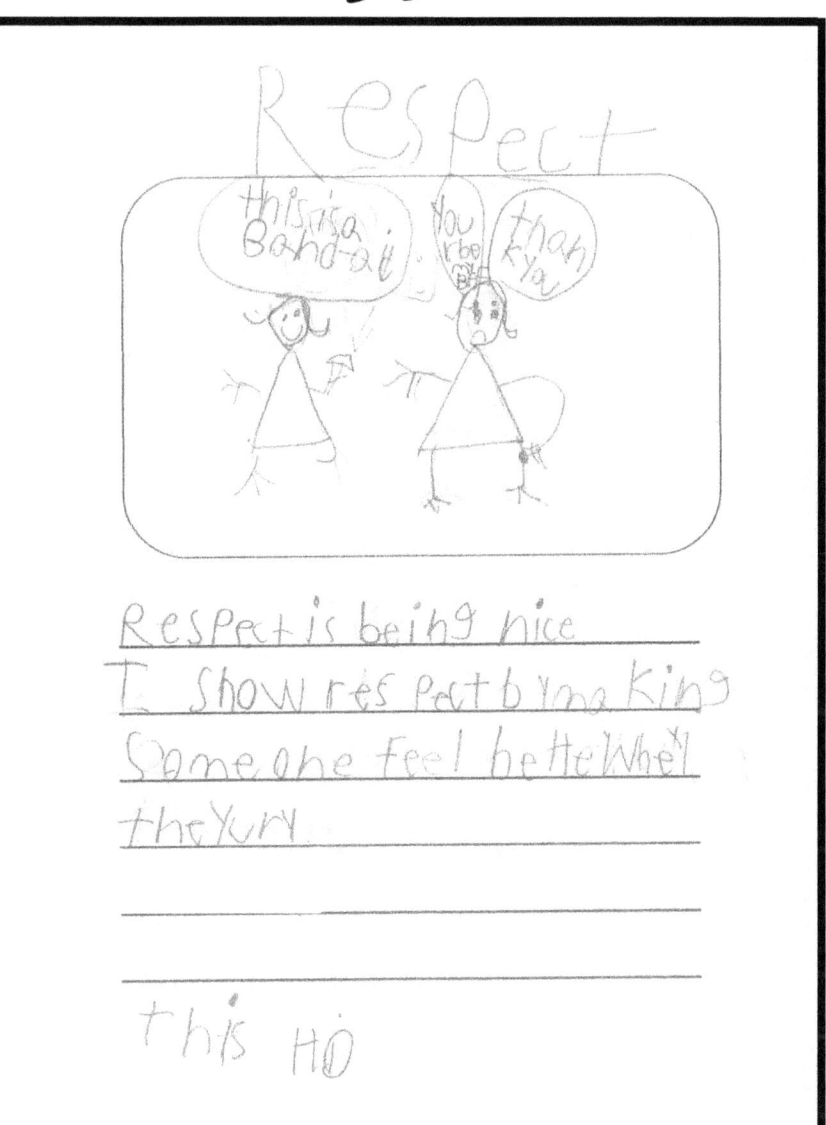

Grade: 1st Grade

Gabriel

Respect means doing hands and eyes as being told.
by Gabriel

Male
Grade: 1st Grade

Frank

respect means to be caring.
I show respect by sharing

by: Frank

Male
Grade: 1st Grade

Hildaieli

Respect means be kind. I show respect by helping people up when they fall.
By = Hidaieli

Female
Grade: 1st Grade

Iman

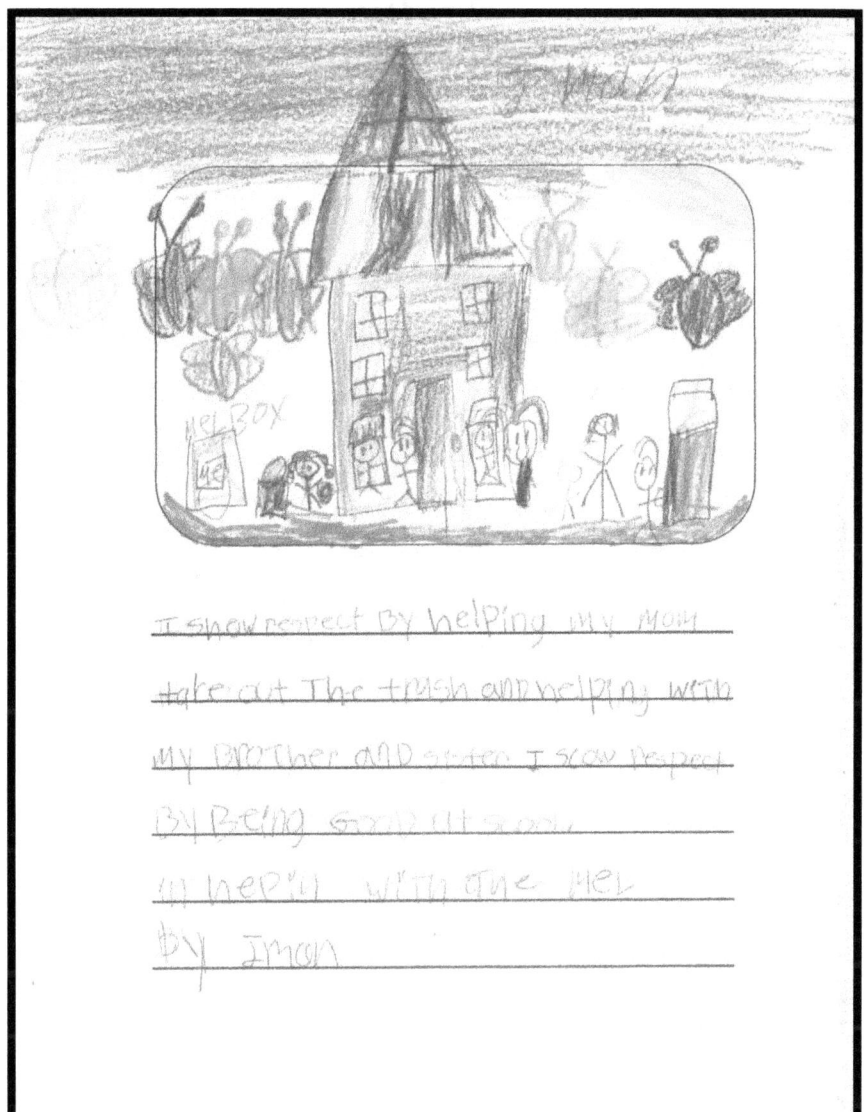

I show respect by helping my mom take out the trash and helping with my brother and sister. I show respect by being good at school and helping with the mel.

by Iman

Female
Grade: 1st Grade

Jaidyn

Respect means listening to people and doing what your parents say. You have to respect everyone at home, at school, and the park.

by: Jaidyn

Female
Grade: 1st Grade

Jamiion

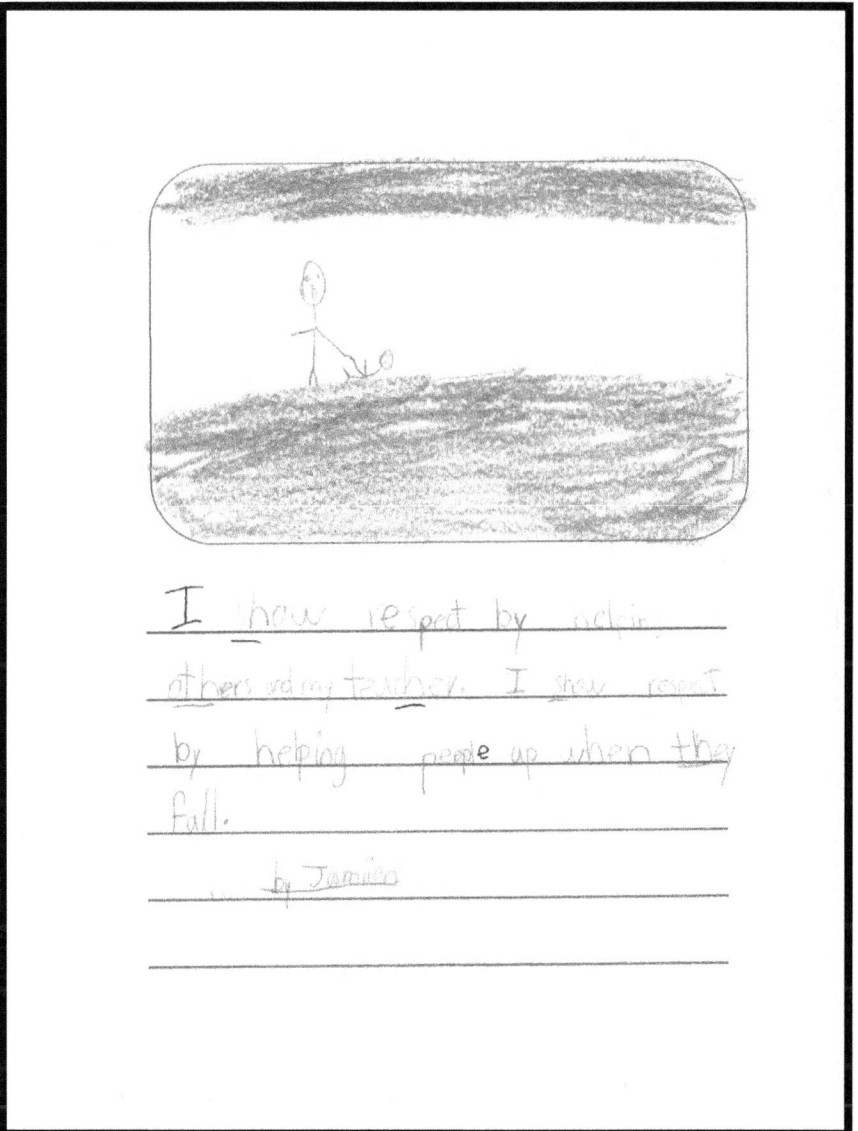

I show respect by ackin others ra my teacher. I show respect by helping people up when they fall.

by Jamiion

Male
Grade: 1st Grade

Janilah

I respect my mom and my dad a my famle. I will all ways respect my famle iIito they rspet the I will respect them. I love my famle.
By Janilah

Female
Grade: 1st Grade

Winners are Respectful

Jayden B.

I show respect by listening to my teacher, means sayin people to not be bad
by Jayden B

Male
Grade: 1st Grade

Jayden M.

I show Respect by listening to my mum. when I get in troble I take the consequence. Someone who is a hero is Respectful and somone who does get mad and talks back to the techer is not Respectful. Respect mean to be kind.

By. Jayden

Male
Grade: 1st Grade

Jayla K.

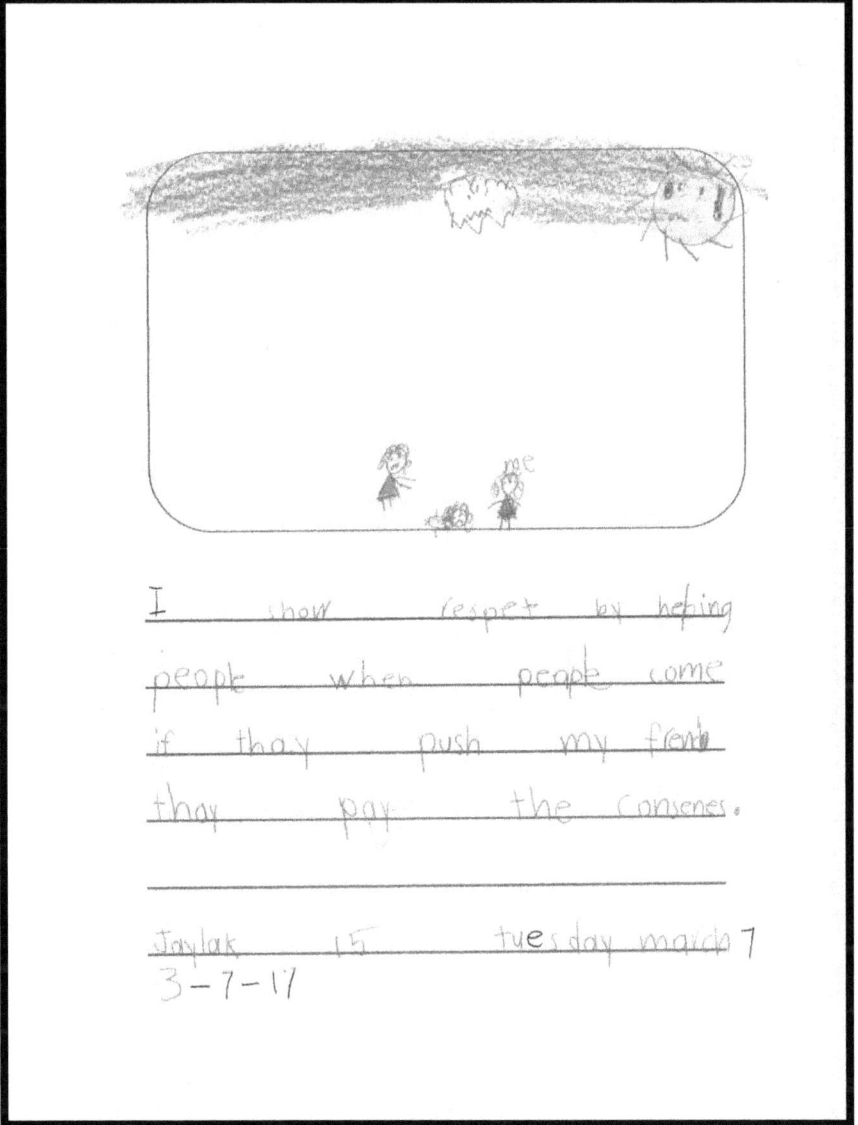

I show respet by heping people when peaple come if thay push my frend thay pay the consenes.

Jaylak 15 tuesday march 7
3-7-17

Female
Grade: 1st Grade

Jayla N.

book *mrs. tees. book*

I Show Respect by listening to my teacher By Jayla N.

I show RESPect by listening to my teacher and my entire family. I also help my teacher.
by Jayla
I u oll

Female
Grade: 1st Grade

Jessica

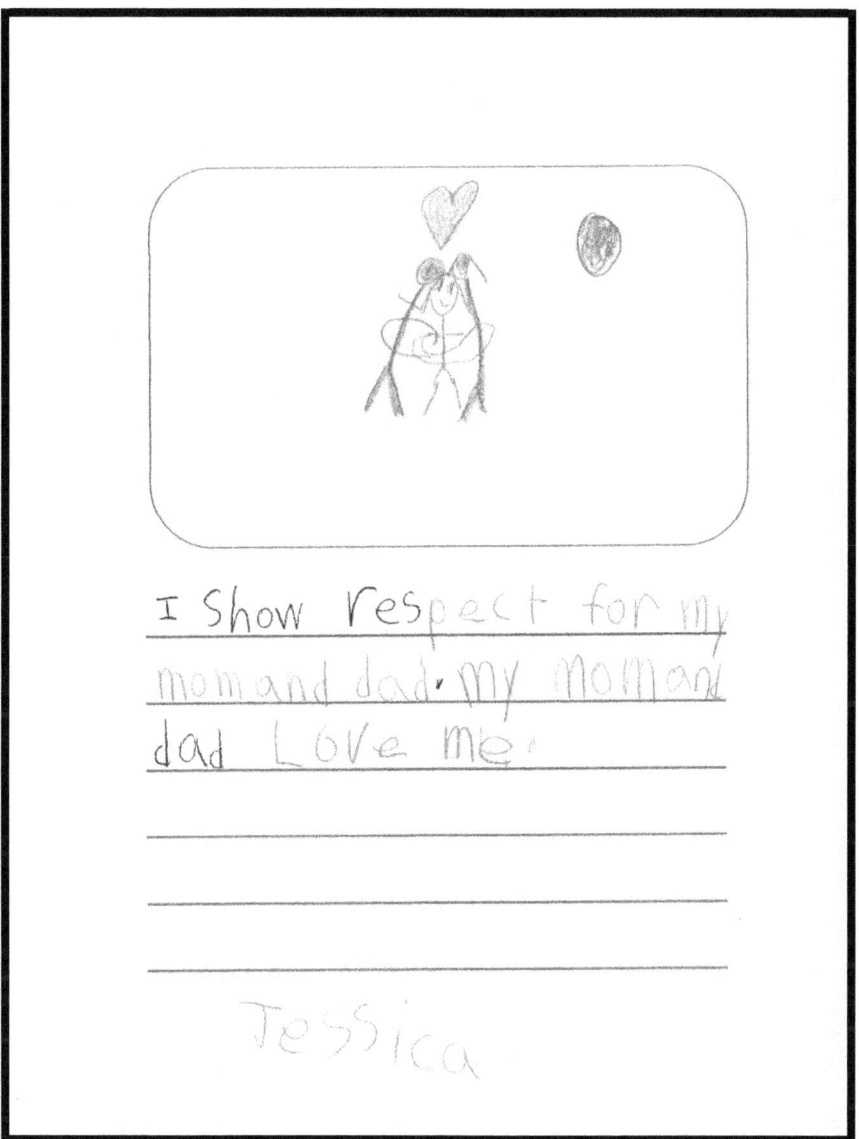

I show respect for my mom and dad. my mom and dad Love me.

Jessica

Female
Grade: 1st Grade

Kai'Asia

I show respect by listening and I show respect by clipping up and makeing my teacher prous. I show respect by sharing my snack and makeing smart choices and helping pepole up.

To Kaiasia from ms.ters   By Kaisia

Female
Grade: 1st Grade

Kamari

I show respect by heleing my mum and dad bake a cake. Respecthelping my friends.
by Kamari

Female
Grade: 1st Grade

Kingston

BY KINGSTON
I show respect
BY LiSTENING
AND NOT TALKSMAt
to MY MoM ANd dad
AND I CL) eup that shows M y Mom
AND dAd that I caN get oN the
NeClAC AND oN blue

Male

Grade: 1st Grade

Ky'lah

I respect my mom.
I respect my dad.
I listen to my sister.

By Ky'lah

Female
Grade: 1st Grade

Lariah

Respect is being nice to others!

I Lariah

Female
Grade: 1st Grade

Winners are Respectful

Layla

I show respect by listening to my Dad and my teachers. Respect means to help othes.

by Layla

Female
Grade: 1st Grade

London

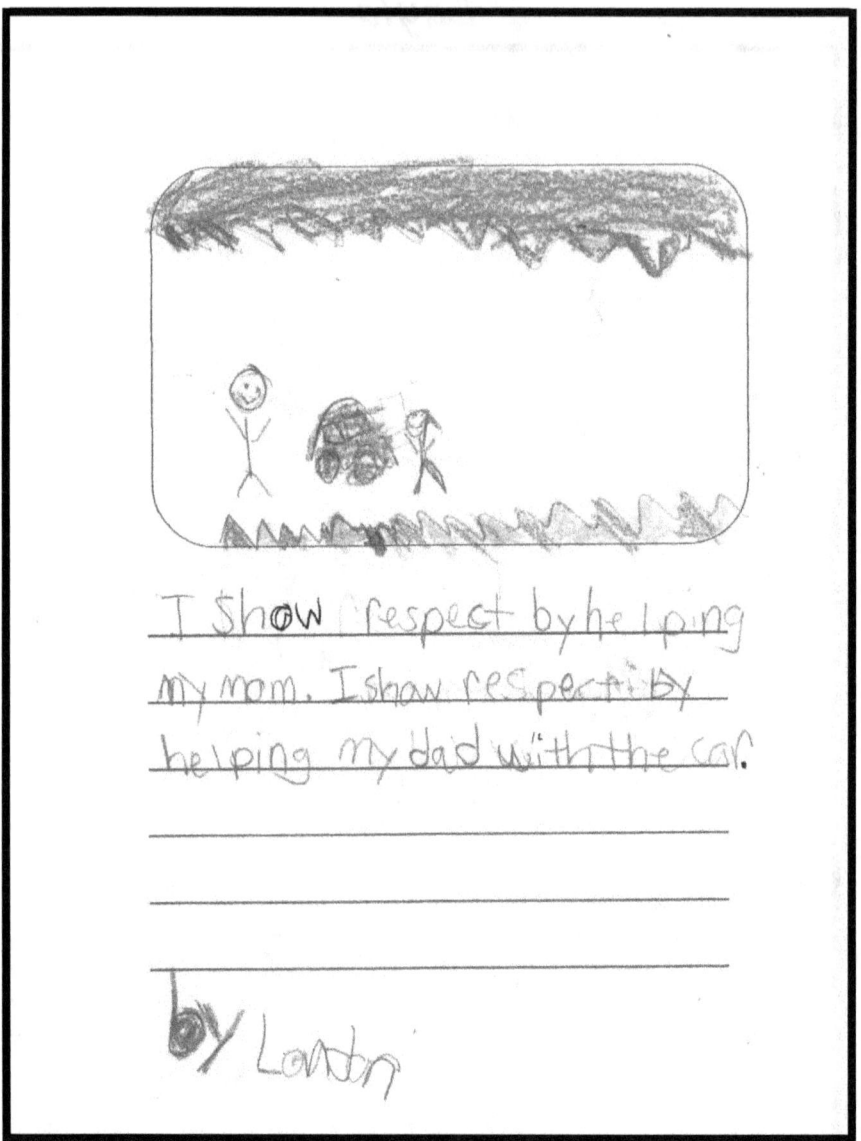

I show respect by helping my mom. I show respect by helping my dad with the car.

by London

Female
Grade: 1st Grade

Anonynous

Relpe 4 ne putoh
K ...

Female
Grade: 1st Grade

Malakhei

respect listening
means rules
I show respect
you teacher in the
respect means to
He bld in because him
by Malakhi

Male
Grade: 1st Grade

Anonynous

Respect means being kind. I show respect by being considate.

Male
Grade: 1st Grade

Monicsha

Respect means to help people iisent.

by Monicsha

Female
Grade: 1st Grade

Nacarra

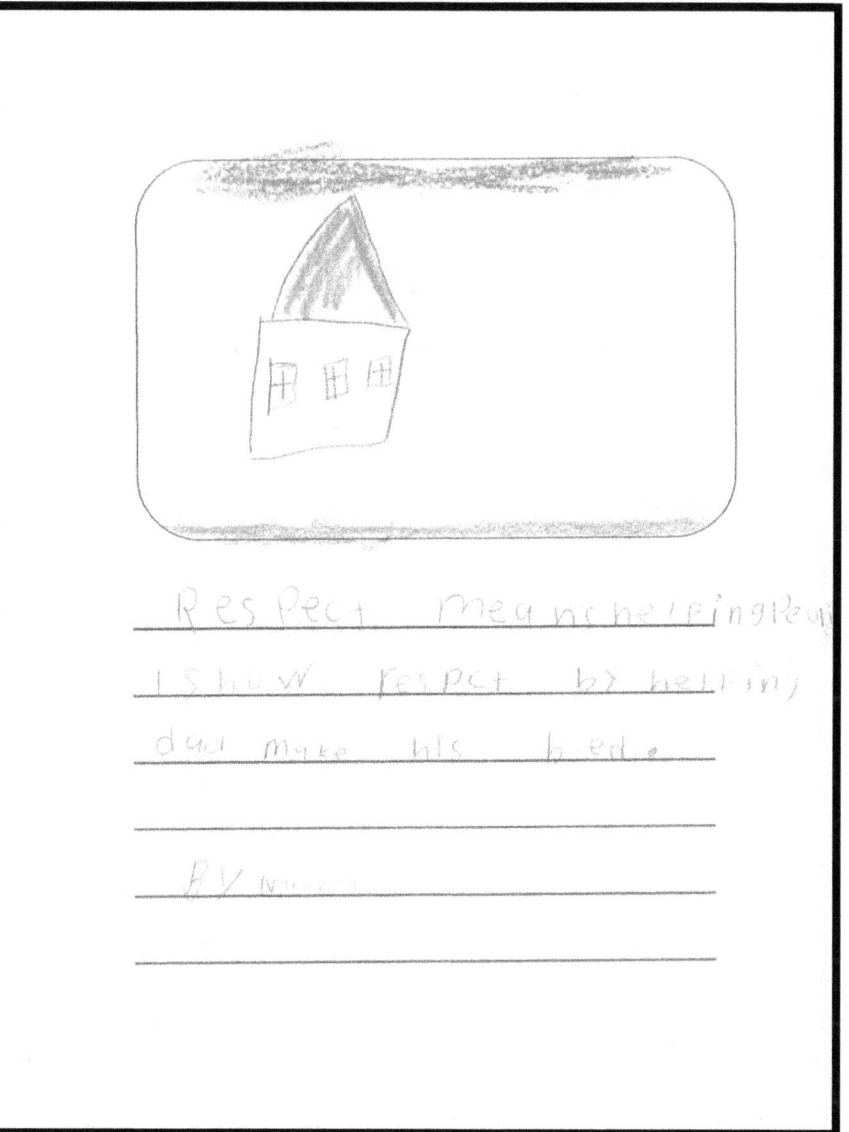

Respect mean helping people. I show respect by helping dad make his bed.

By Nacarra

Female
Grade: 1st Grade

Natalie

I show repect bu listening to my teacher, people, mom, dad the rules. I follow Directions quickly and quietty.

Natalie   3/7/17

Female
Grade: 1st Grade

Winners are Respectful

Paulina

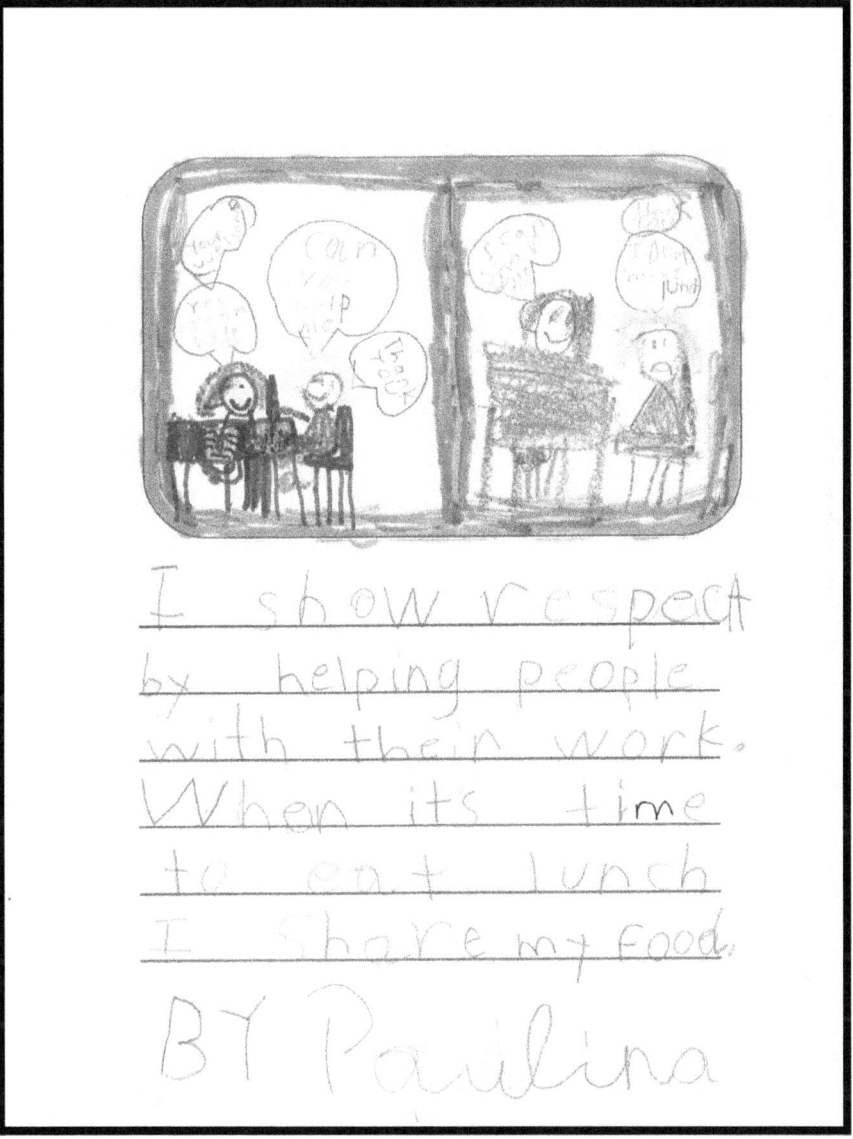

I show respect by helping people with their work. When its time to eat lunch I share my food.
BY Paulina

Female
Grade: 1st Grade

Anonymous

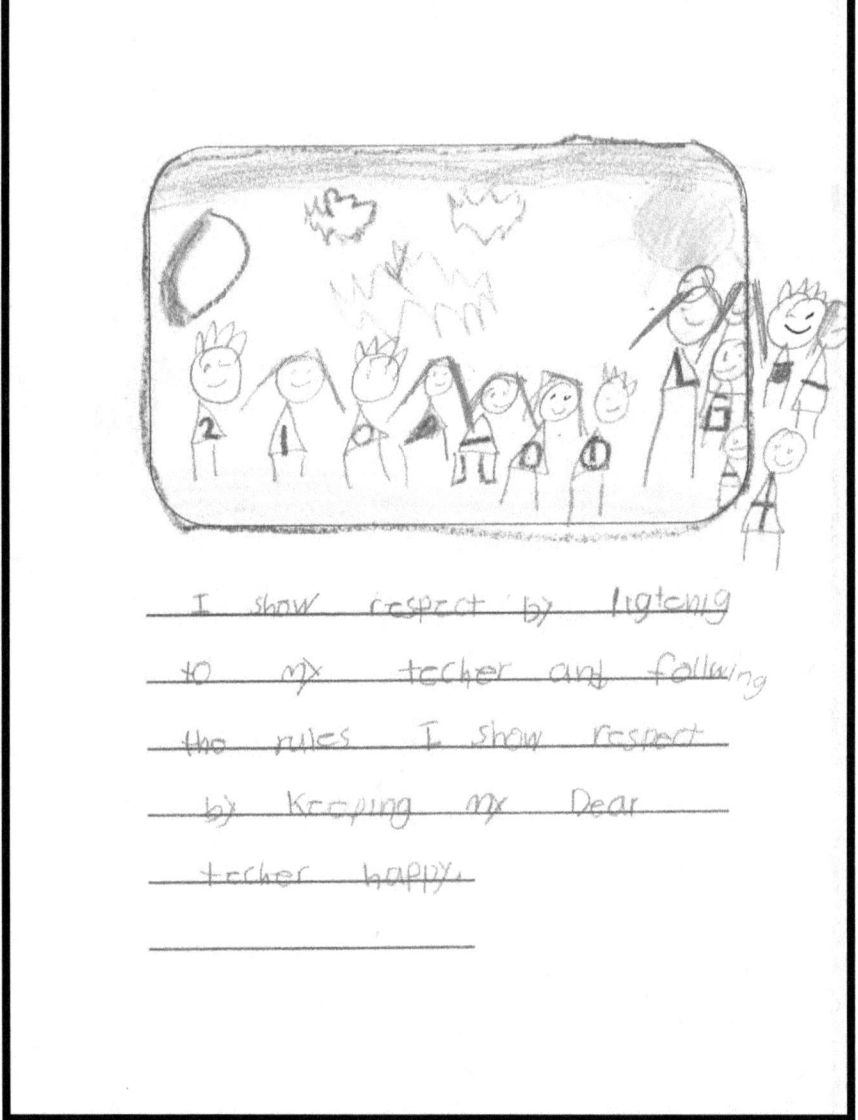

I show respect by ligtenig to my techer and follwing tho rules I show respect by kreping my Dear techer happy.

Female
Grade: 1ˢᵗ Grade

Sasha

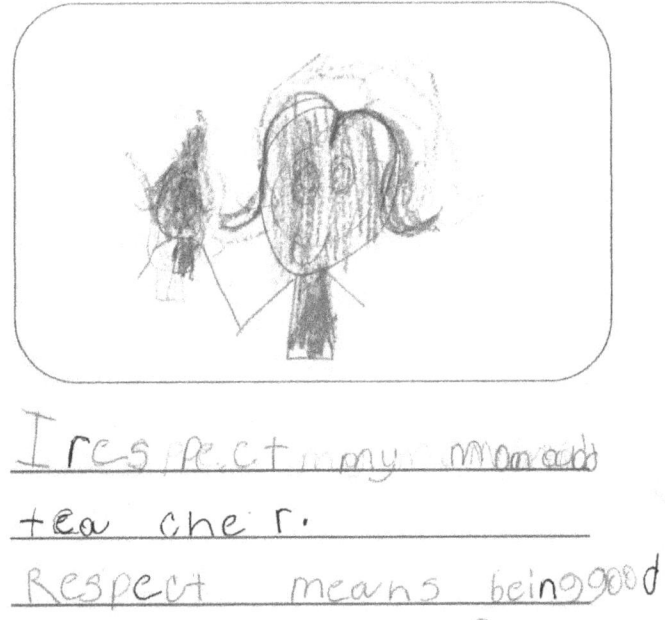

I respect my mom and teacher.
Respect means being good to my family Dads Bn sasha

Female
Grade: 1st Grade

Sophia

I will listen to my mom and my sister every day. and I Love my mom and my sister.

by Sophia

Female
Grade: 1st Grade

Tacarra

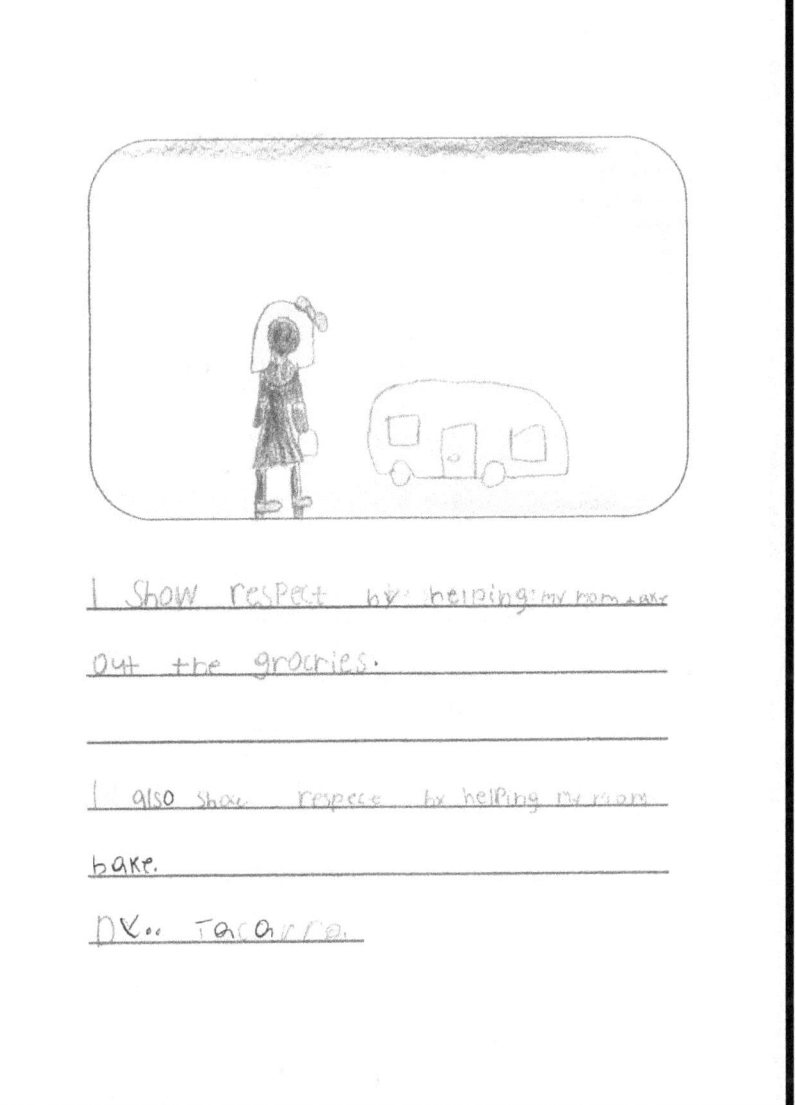

I show respect by helping my mom take out the groceries.

I also show respect by helping my mom bake.

By Tacarra.

Female
Grade: 1st Grade

Anonynous

Respect means listening to your mom and dad. Respect means not yell at the teacher.

Female
Grade: 1st Grade

Toree

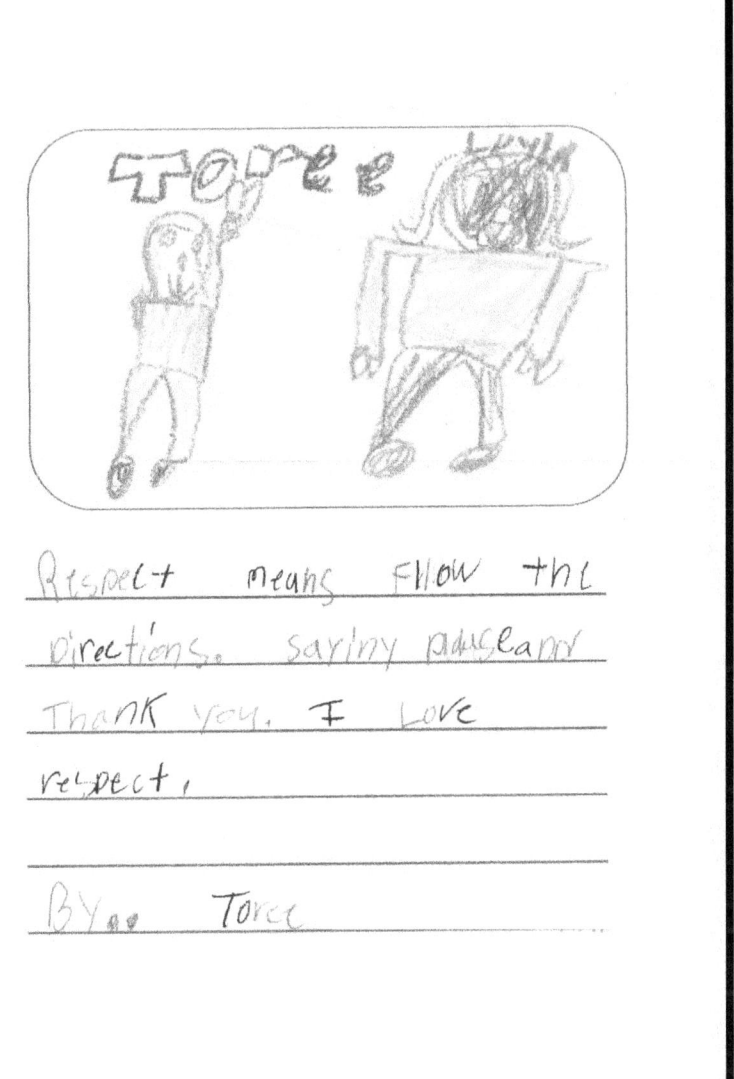

Respect means Fllow the directions, saying please and Thank you. I Love respect,

By.. Toree

Female
Grade: 1st Grade

Trevor

Respect is to listen to your techer follow direchons quickly. helping is to Listes to you teacher helping u thr pepol.

by
Name Trevor

Male

Grade: 1st Grade

Anonynous

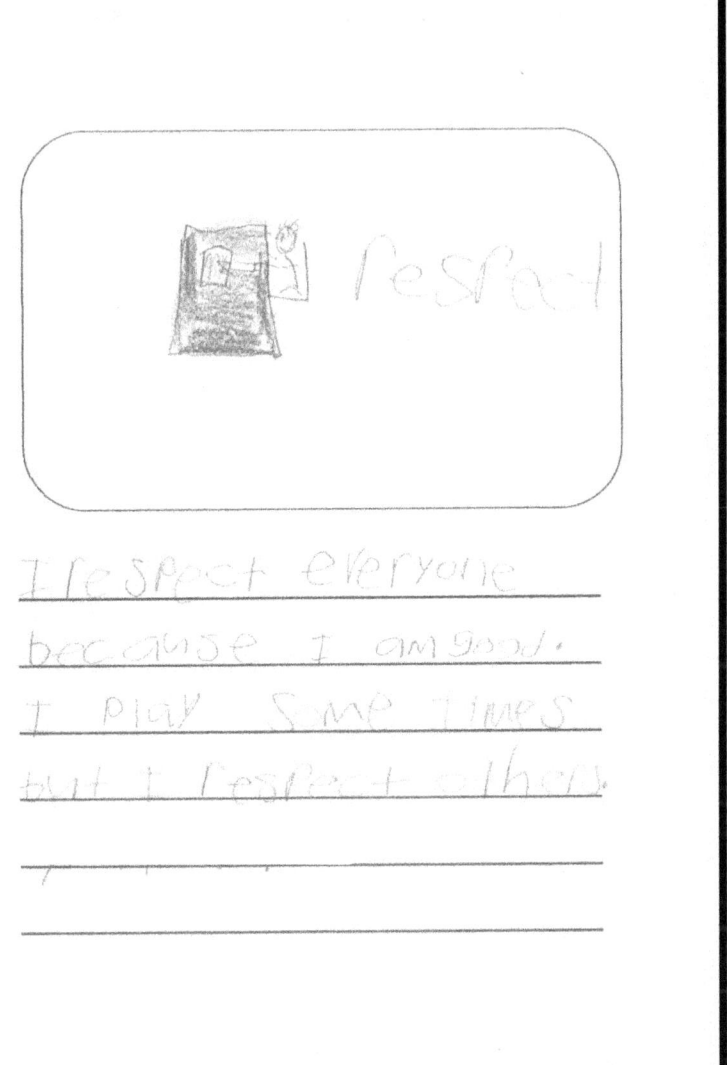

I respect everyone because I am good. I play some times but I respect others.

Male
Grade: 1st Grade

Anonynous

Respect means saying please and thank you. and following my moms rules

Male
Grade: 1st Grade

Zion

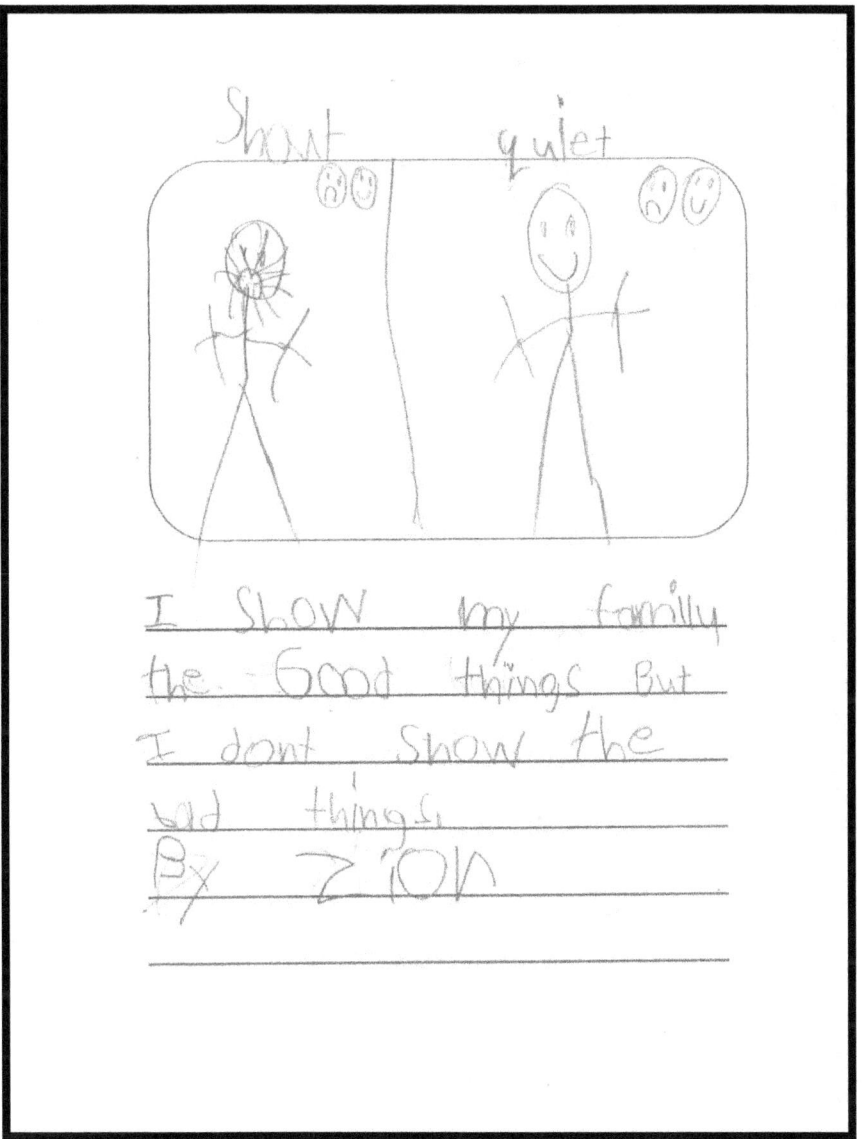

I show my familly the Good things But I dont show the bad things. By Zion

Male
Grade: 1st Grade

Zoey

1. I show respect to me mom and dad.
2. I show respect to my school.
3. I show respect by listening.
4. I show my family.
   I show respect to people.
   by Zoey

Female
Grade: 1st Grade

CHAPTER 3
Castro

Aaliyah

I was at school and I was being good. I am respectful because I do all of my work. I listen to my good teacher. I get good grades. I am nice to my friends because when they need help I help them.

Female
Grade: 2nd Grade

Aaron *(Part 1)*

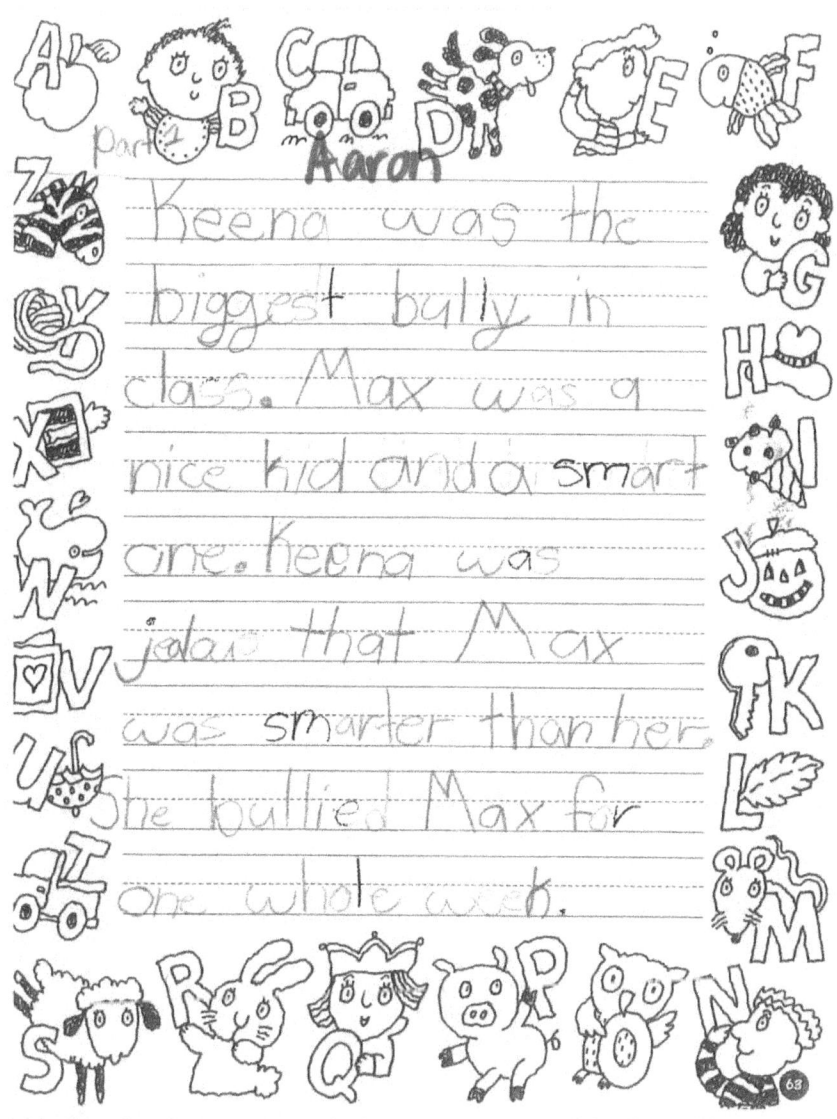

Aaron

Keena was the biggest bully in class. Max was a nice kid and a smart one. Keena was jelas that Max was smarter than her. She bullied Max for one whole week.

Male

Grade: 2nd Grade

Aaron (Part 2)

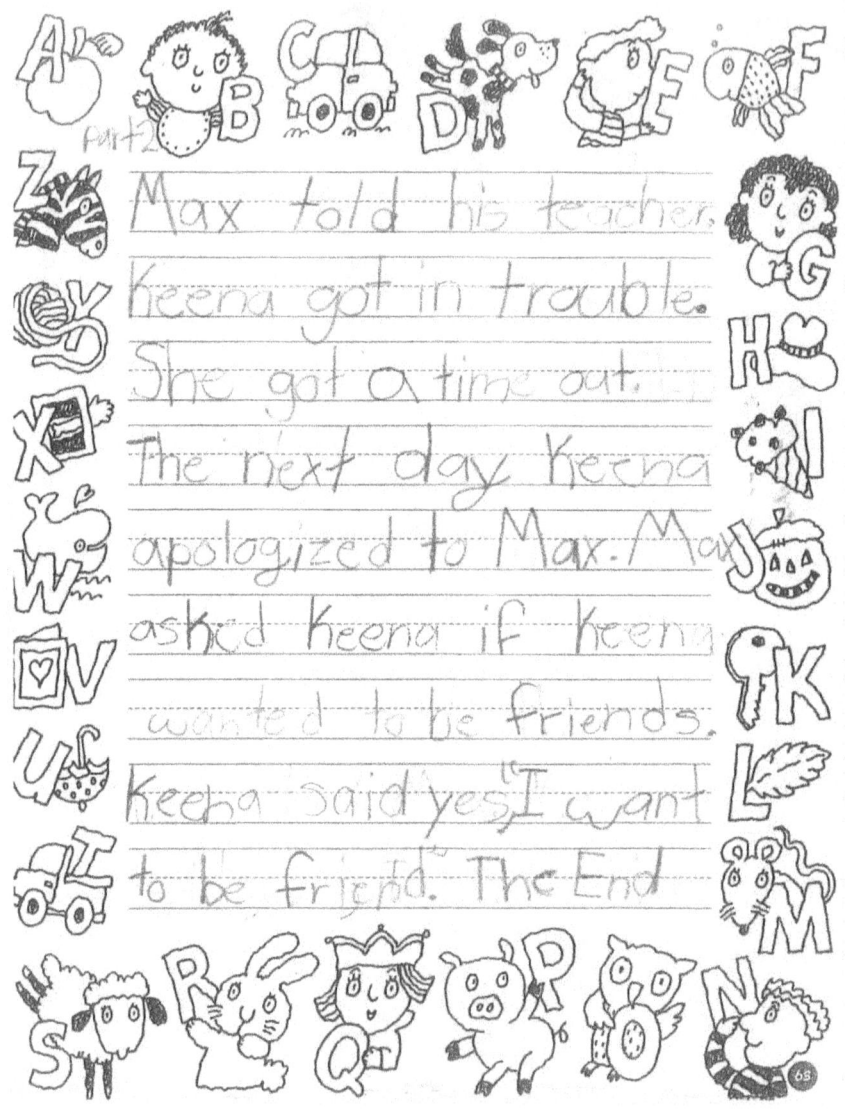

Max told his teacher, Keena got in trouble. She got a time out. The next day Keena apologized to Max. Max asked Keena if Keena wanted to be friends. Keena said "yes I want to be friend." The End

Male
Grade: 2nd Grade

Alondra (Part 1)

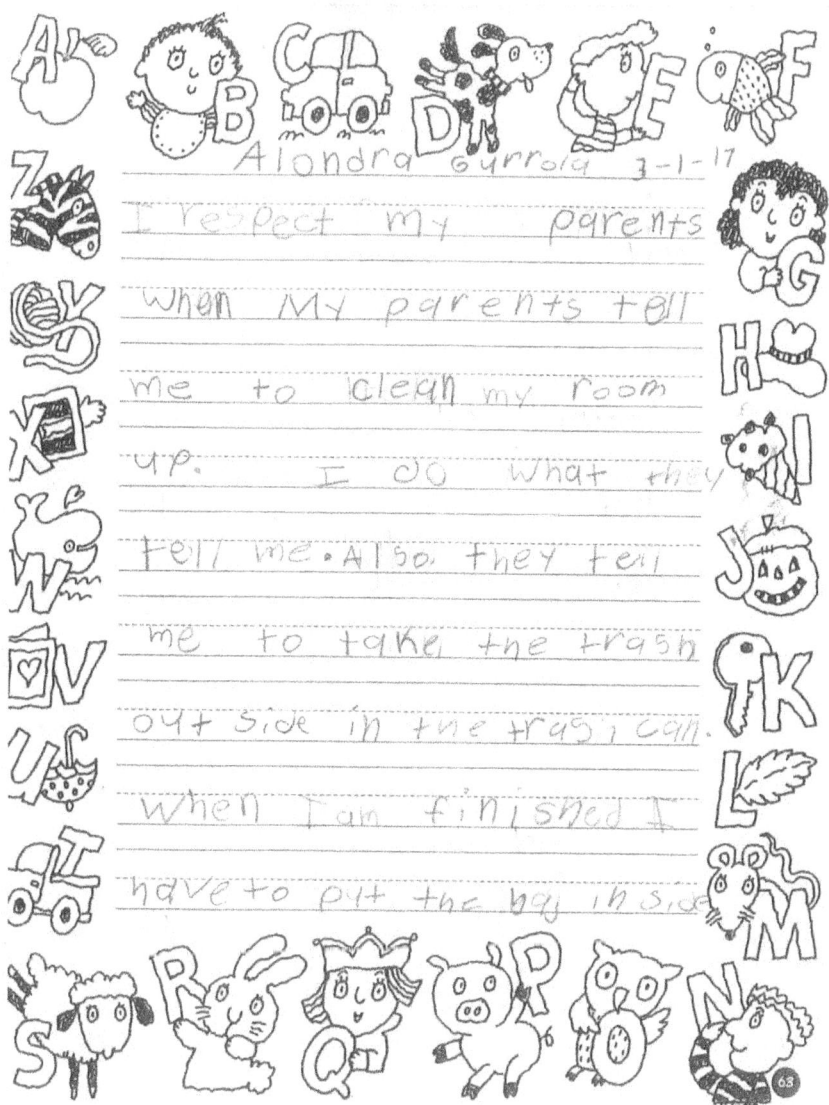

Alondra Gurrola 3-1-17

I respect my parents when my parents tell me to clean my room up. I do what they tell me. Also they tell me to take the trash outside in the trash can. When I am finished I have to put the bag inside

Female
Grade: 2nd Grade

Alondra (Part 2)

the trash can. When I finish I have to help my mom to clean the kitchen. When I finish helping my mom I help my dad to learn how to speak English. When I finish cleaning my house I go to sleep.

Female
Grade: 2nd Grade

Andres

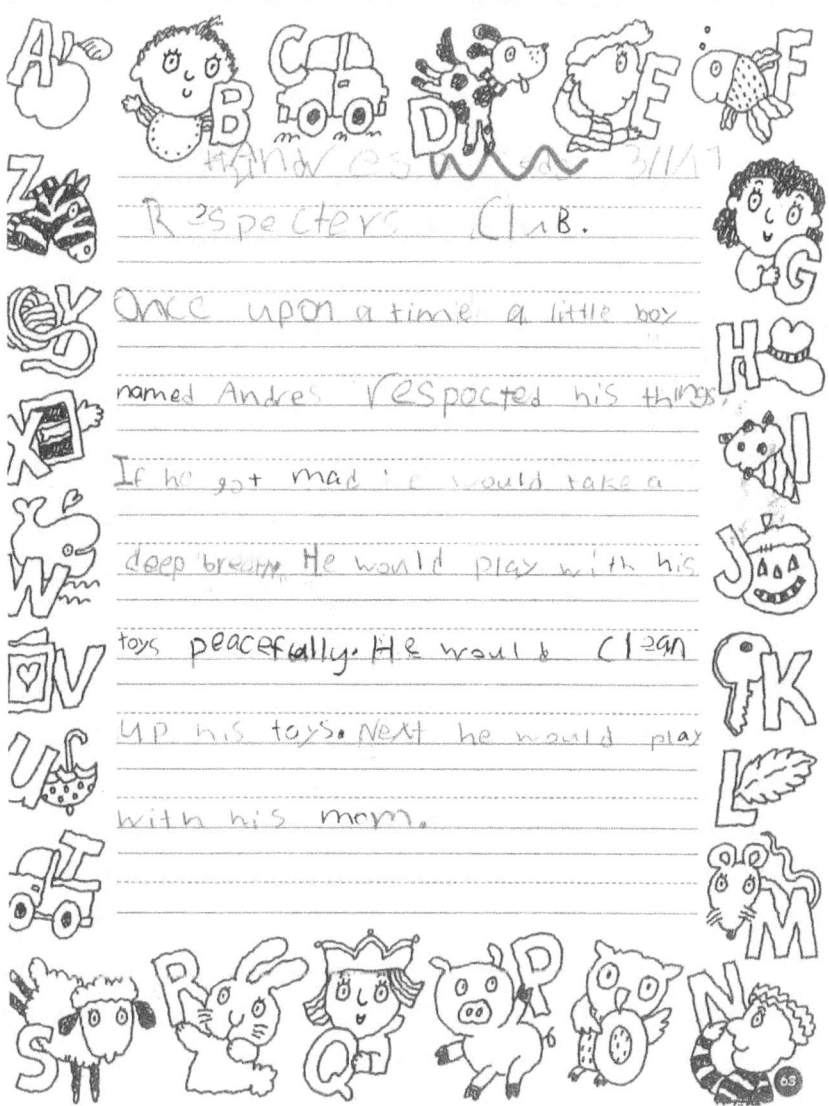

Respecters Club.

Once upon a time a little boy named Andres respected his things. If he got mad he would take a deep breath. He would play with his toys peacefully. He would clean up his toys. Next he would play with his mom.

Male
Grade: 2nd Grade

Derek

Me and my friends show
Respect to everybody, we
Do not hurt anyone I will be
Respectful to my mom and dad.

Male
Grade: 2nd Grade

Winners are Respectful

Donavon (Part 1)

Once upon time a girl named Jane loved her family. She respected them by listening and obying her rules. Jane her mom and dad went to fish. Jane watched the work. Jane caught 12 fish. Her dad caught

Male
Grade: 2nd Grade

Donavon (Part 2)

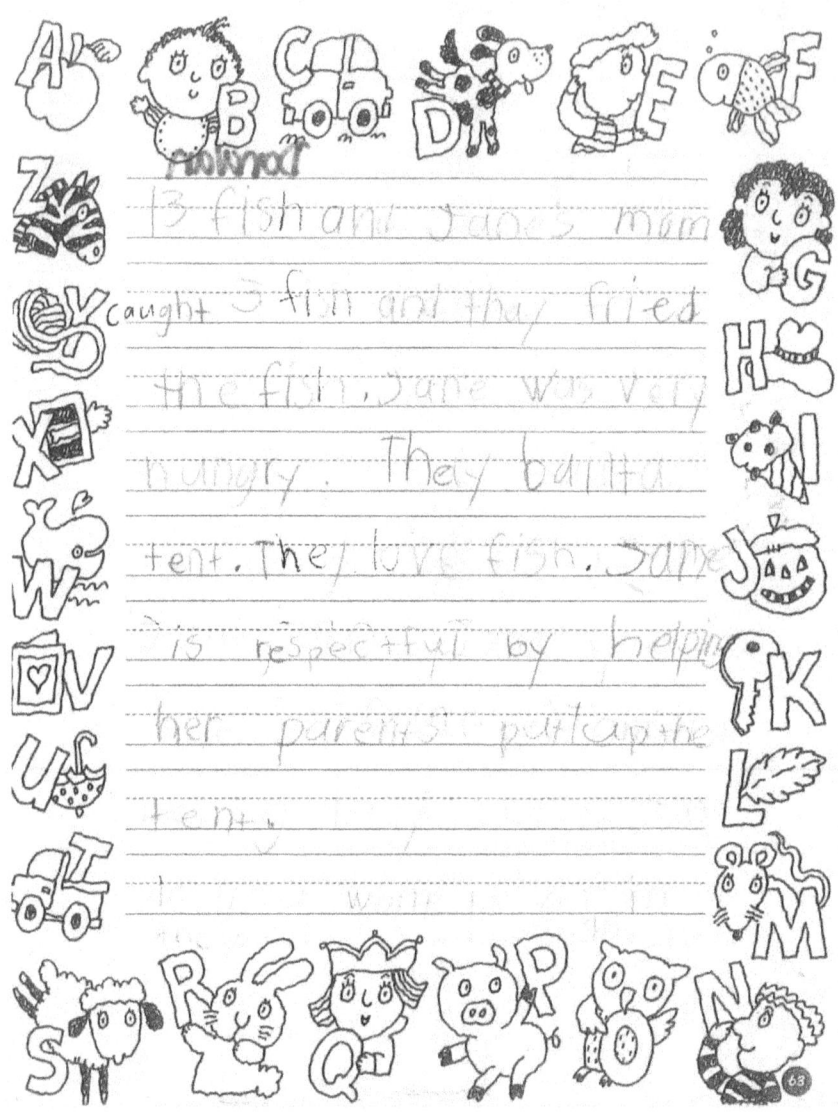

13 fish and Jane's mom caught 3 fish and they fried the fish. Jane was very hungry. They built a tent. They love fish. Jane is respectful by helping her parents put up the tent.

Male
Grade: 2nd Grade

Donnaven

I RESPECT my teacher because she is a grownup. She teaches kids because she is smart. I show RESPECT to my teacher by Listening.

Male
Grade: 2nd Grade

Emelia (Part 1)

Title: I love respect
One day, their was a teacher named Ms. ba.
She was in a class with kids and their were rules. Next day, their were kids talking back And not showing any respect or using manners.

Female
Grade: 2nd Grade

Emelia (Part 2)

They have to do a Respect paper. so they will respect to the teacher and the classroom. The Next day, They were respecting the free play teacher. And they had free play and they were

Female
Grade: 2nd Grade

Emelia (Part 3)

respect the other kids.

Female
Grade: 2nd Grade

Hannah (Part 1)

Once upon a time there was a girl named Samantha. Her and her friend came up to me and said bad words. I told her to be respectful. Then she came up to me and did it again. She hurt my feelings so I went in the bathroom. All of sudden she

Female
Grade: 2nd Grade

Hannah (Part 2)

came in and said sorry.
So me, Samantha and I became
friend forever. The End

Female
Grade: 2nd Grade

Winners are Respectful

Haylee *(Part 1)*

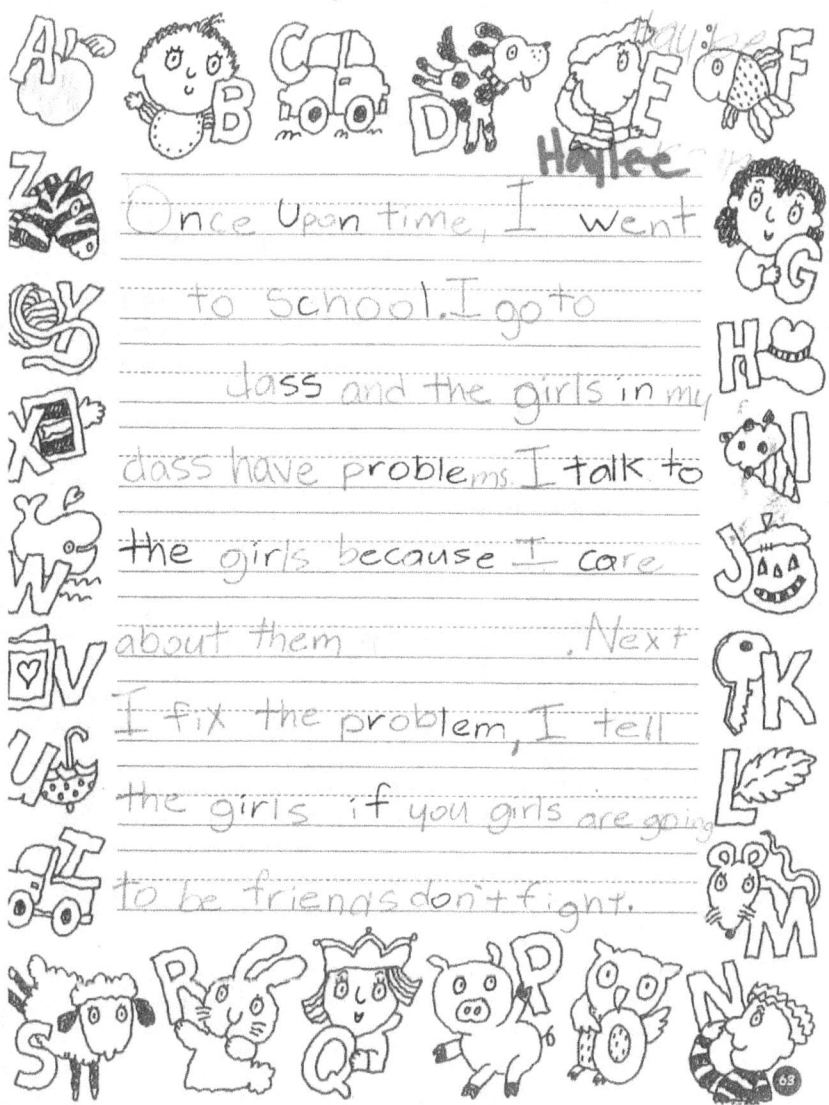

Once Upon time, I went to school. I go to class and the girls in my class have problems. I talk to the girls because I care about them. Next I fix the problem, I tell the girls if you girls are going to be friends don't fight.

Female
Grade: 2nd Grade

Haylee (Part 2)

On the next day the girls got chips. The girls ate the chips and the girls were done eating the chips. Then the girls threw the trash down the floor. The teacher got the girls and the girls were crying. Their mom got mad at the girls. The End.

Female
Grade: 2nd Grade

Haylee (Part 3)

if you are mean to people that not good.

Female
Grade: 2nd Grade

Isabella

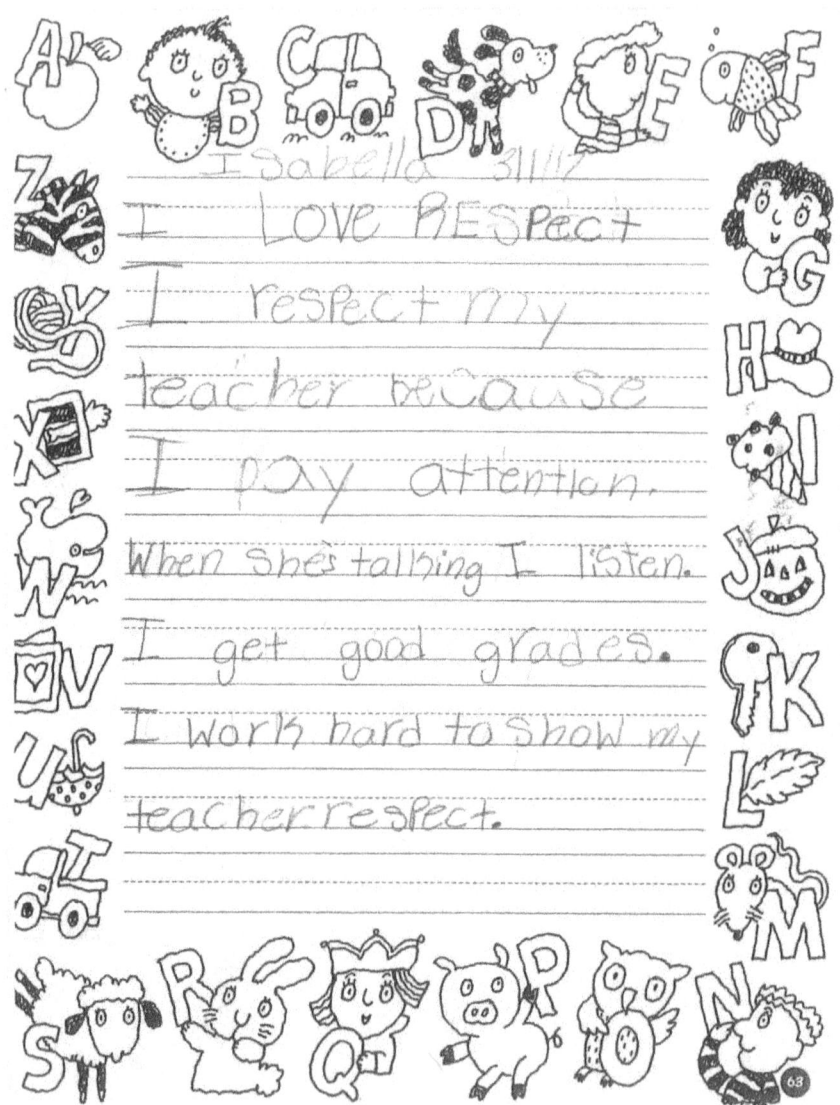

I LOVE RESPect
I respect my teacher because I pay attention. When she's talking I listen. I get good grades. I work hard to show my teacher respect.

Female
Grade: 2nd Grade

Keishawn (Part 1)

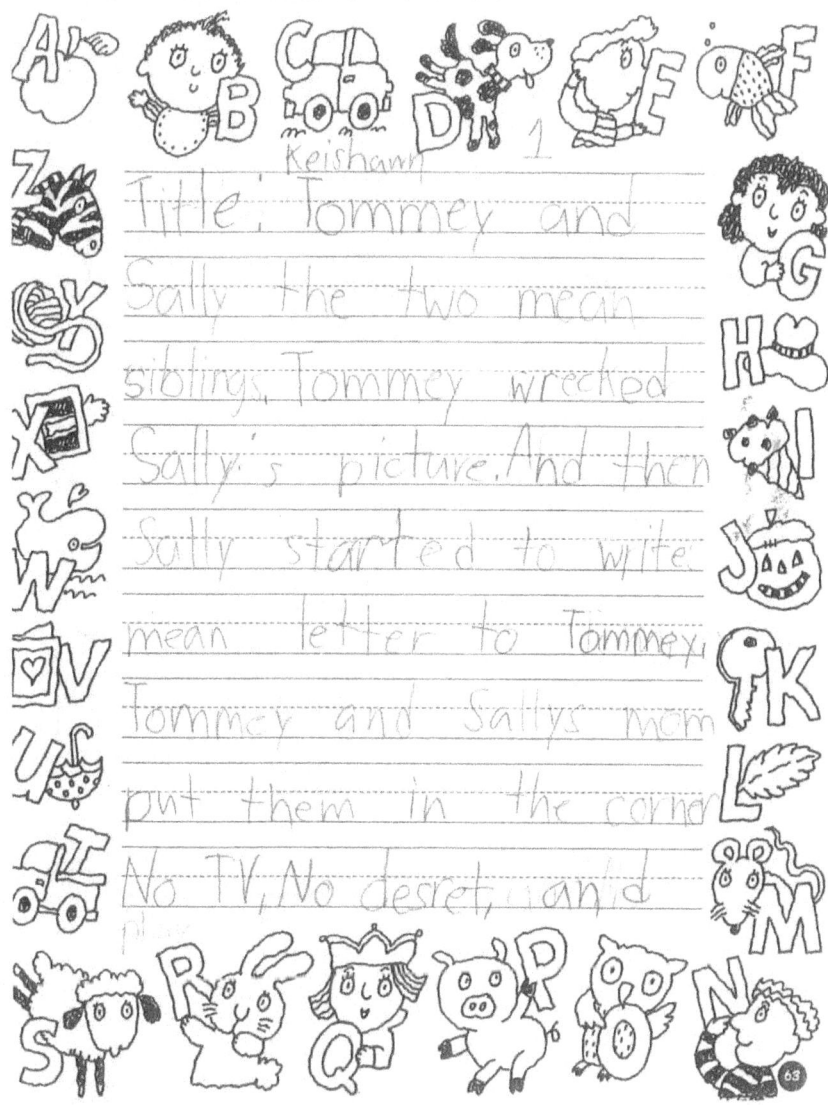

Title: Tommey and Sally the two mean siblings. Tommey wrecked Sally's picture. And then Sally started to write mean letter to Tommey. Tommey and Sallys mom put them in the corner No TV, No desret, and

Male
Grade: 2nd Grade

Keishawn (Part 2)

Male
Grade: 2nd Grade

Winners are Respectful

Keishawn *(Part 3)*

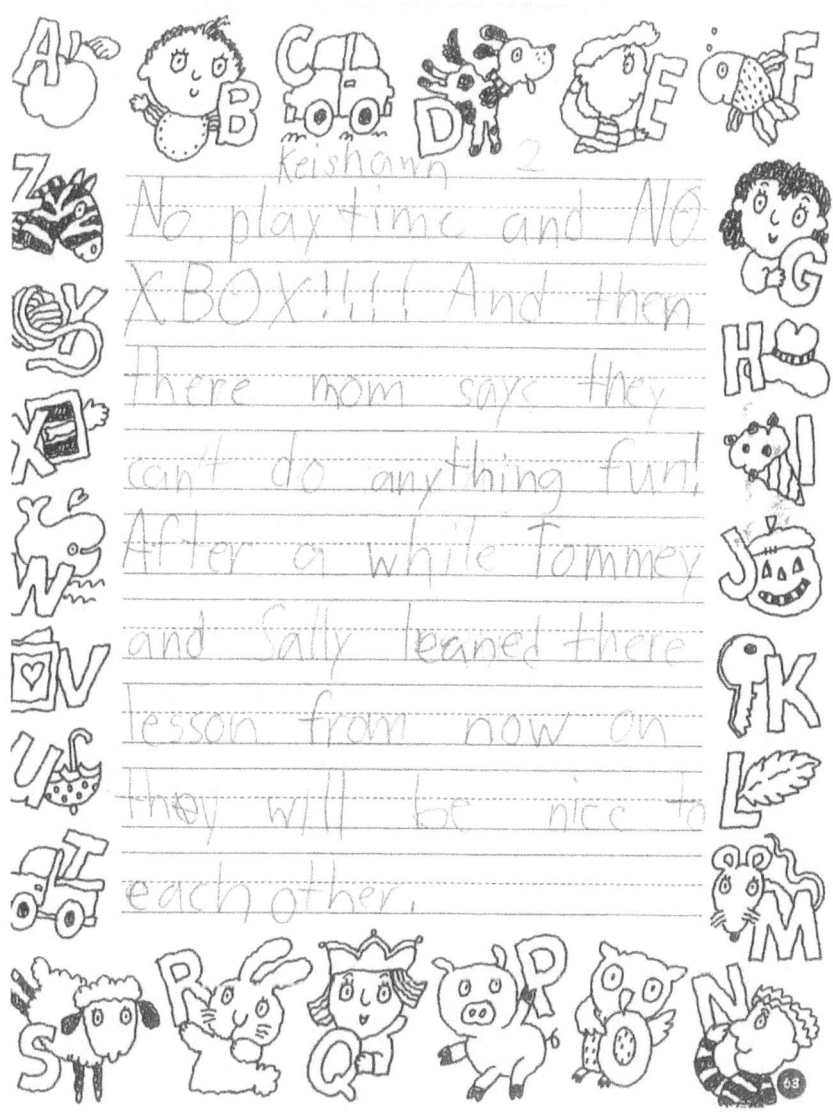

Keishawn 2
No play time and NO
XBOX!!! And then
There mom says they
can't do anything fun!
After a while Tommey
and Sally leaned there
lesson from now on
they will be nice to
each other.

Male
Grade: 2nd Grade

Makailee (Part 1)

I was always disrespectful to my brother. One time I pushed him off his own bed when he was asleep. I yelled at him because he did not give me my food. I kicked my brother in the leg one time.

Female
Grade: 2nd Grade

Winners are Respectful

Makailee (Part 2)

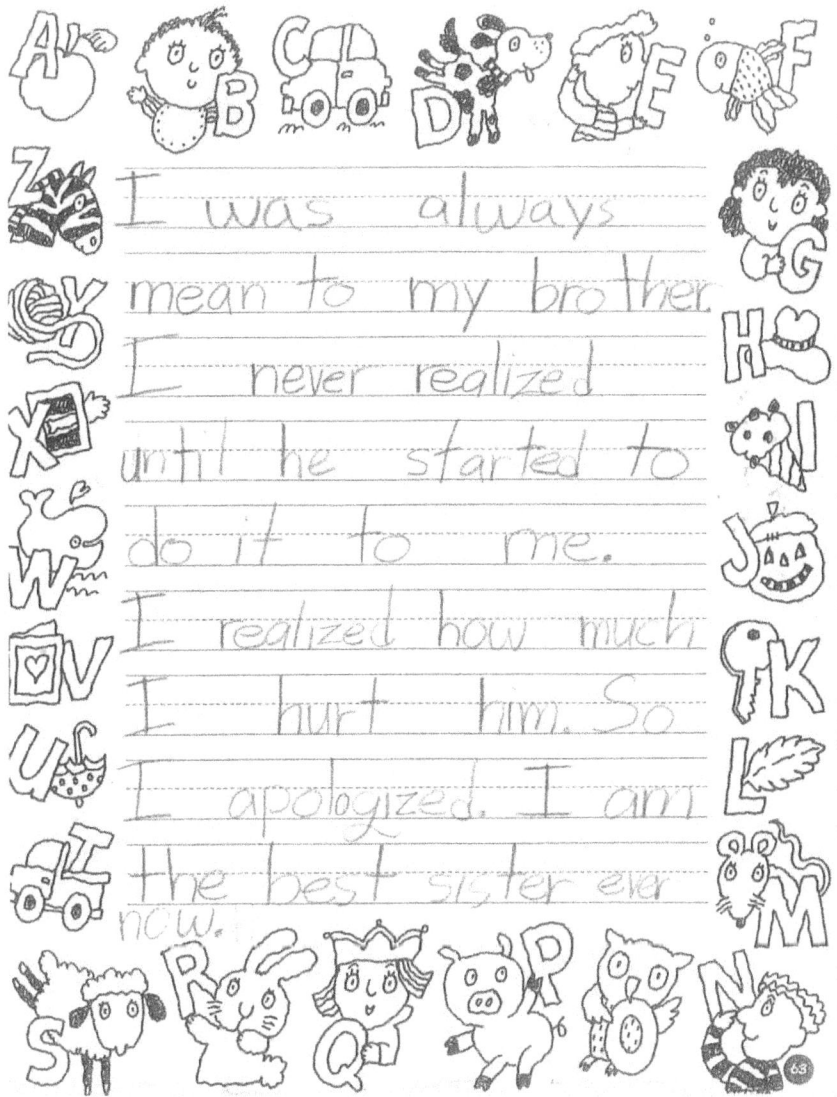

I was always mean to my brother. I never realized until he started to do it to me. I realized how much I hurt him. So I apologized. I am the best sister ever now.

Female
Grade: 2nd Grade

Najriyah (Part 1)

Once upon a time there was a boy named Doug. He always listens to the teacher and he always gets candy from the teacher. He has a lot of friends. He has ten friends and I'm one of them. He always plays with

Female
Grade: 2nd Grade

Winners are Respectful

Najriyah (Part 2)

me. He always shares with me
too. He's my bff because he is
respeortcal to me.

Female
Grade: 2nd Grade

Osvaldo (Part 1)

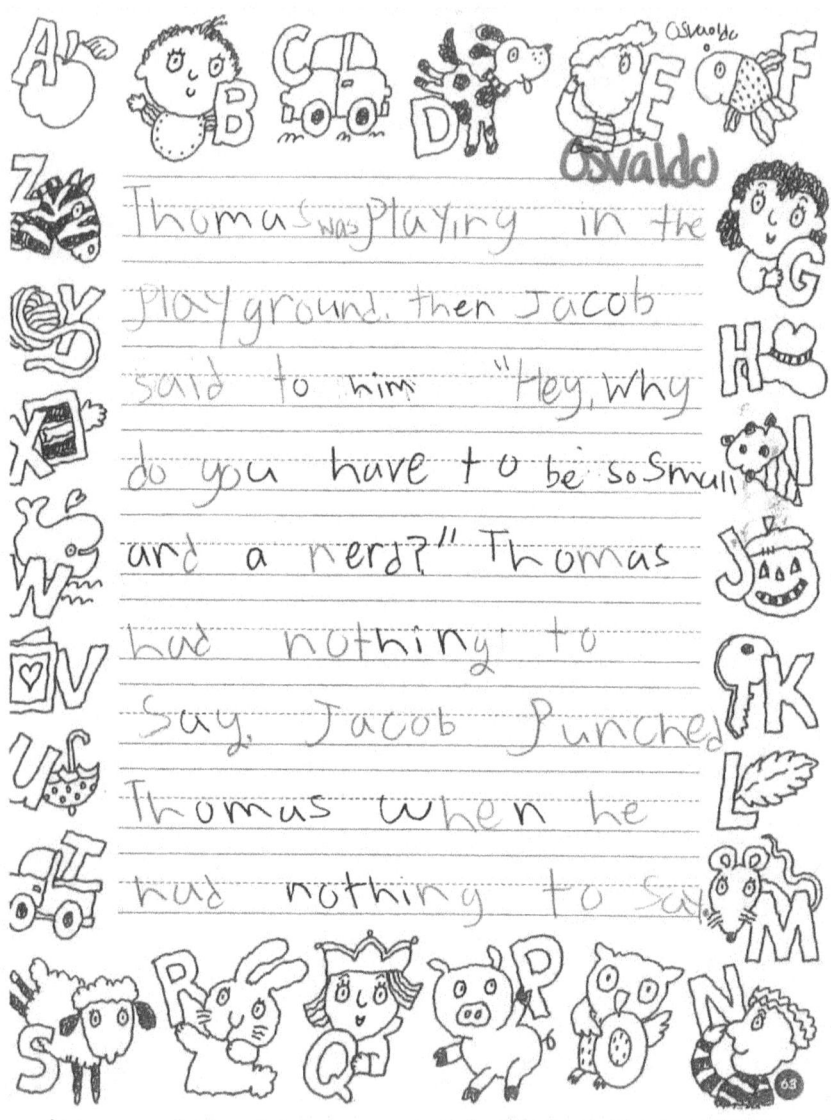

Thomas was playing in the playground. then Jacob said to him "Hey, why do you have to be so small and a nerd?" Thomas had nothing to say. Jacob Punched Thomas when he had nothing to say.

Male
Grade: 2nd Grade

Osvaldo (Part 2)

Thomas fell to the ground when Thomas fell to the ground. Jacob kicked sand at him. Then they went to class. The teacher talked about respect. Jacob learned to stop bullying.

Male
Grade: 2nd Grade

Prophet (Part 1)

One day it was a nice day and there were two boys named Prophet and Max. They ro[pe] schools. They respect people and their parents. They are nice to others. Also, they like to invite people to dinner. They had steak.

Male
Grade: 2nd Grade

Prophet *(Part 2)*

hamburgers, and tacos. For dessert they had cupcakes and a banana split.

Male
Grade: 2nd Grade

Psalms (Part 1)

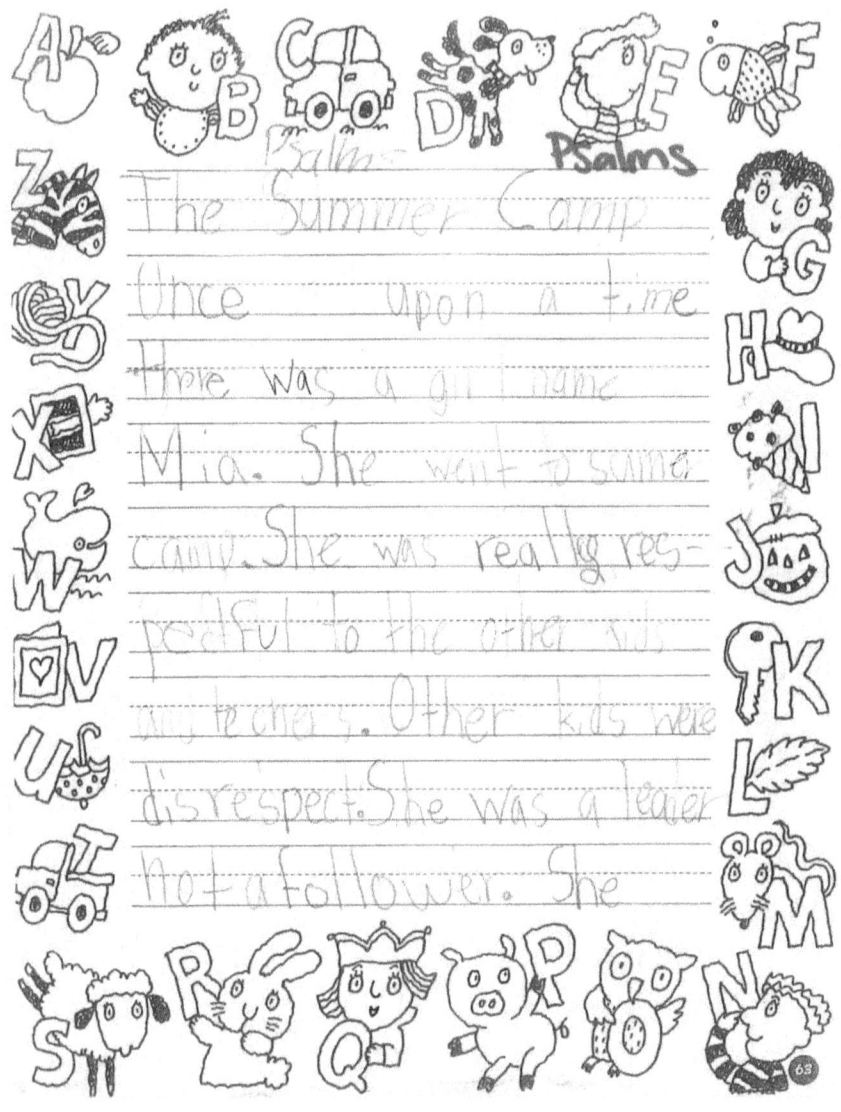

The Summer Camp

Once upon a time there was a girl name Mia. She went to summer camp. She was really respectful to the other kids and teachers. Other kids were disrespect. She was a leader not a follower. She

Female
Grade: 2nd Grade

Psalms (Part 2)

Psalms was helpful to the camp counselors.

Female

Grade: 2nd Grade

Samia

Once there was a 18 year old boy named Hunter. He respected the presidents of the United States of America. He always respects the laws. He also votes for a president. When he visited the white House he was never disrespectful. His dad's name was James Baldwin. They knew Brack obame. There was a happy ending. Rest in peace James Baldwin. The End.

Female
Grade: 2nd Grade

Trezure (Part 1)

On Friday June 25th, Mary went to a restaurant for her birthday. She wants a salad and macarohi and cheese. She did not like it so she decided to throw it at her cousin. Her mom said say sorry Mary. She said sorry to her cousin. Then she realized she was being respectful.

Female
Grade: 2nd Grade

Trezure (Part 2)

Female
Grade: 2nd Grade

Winners are Respectful

Autographs

Autographs

Autographs

Autographs

Affirmative Expression would like to congratulate the Life Source Scholars for completing

The Anthology Project

and earning the prestigious title of *published authors!*

If you would like to bring **The Anthology Project** to your school, church, program, or organization please contact us!

Affirmative Expression's
Anthology Project
Turning your students into authorpreneurs!
Tierica Berry (Founder)
678.499.4405

Info@AffirmativeExpression.com
www.AffirmativeExpression.com

www.ingramcontent.com/pod-product-compliance
Lightning Source LLC
Chambersburg PA
CBHW071705040426
42446CB00011B/1923